POETRY ALMANAC 2016

Made in 2016
Typeset in Minion Pro & HK Grotesque
Printed by Short Run Press

Cover Design by Chrissy Williams
Star chart from Mag-7 Star Atlas Project by Andrew L. Johnson
With thanks to Josh Bradley for aid with design

poetrybookfair.com | poetrybookfair@gmail.com

Acknowledgments
All works are published here by permission of the respective poets and publishers, who retain the copyright.

Contents

Introduction

Chrissy Williams & Joey Connolly

The landscape of UK poetry, as it often appears to the general public, is shaped and structured by major prizes, broadsheet newspaper reviews and long-established publishers. Perhaps it's always been the case, or perhaps it's truer now than ever, but behind the curtain of the mainstream press there is an incredibly broad, deep world of poetry, vibrant and singing in every area of the country. The book you're reading now is the only publication which sets out to document, map and mine that world. We hope it is the first of many.

This almanac offers a unique snapshot across contemporary UK poetry publishers. It democratically lays out information about each one and lets them (in almost all cases) speak for themselves. We are enormously grateful to all the publishers who have contributed to this volume, both in terms of listings and poems. We are also very grateful to have your support, as we want the Poetry Book Fair to keep going, and get bigger and better, organically, every year. We sometimes get asked why we keep doing it, and the simple answer is – we think it needs doing. Newcomers to poetry need more ways to get a sense of how extensive the landscape is, and old hands need to keep abreast of new publishers and new poems.

Charles Boyle of CB editions (featured in this almanac), founded the first Poetry Book Fair in 2011. He was assisted by Chrissy Williams, who subsequently took over the running of the Fair and is now Director, with Joey Connolly as Manager. Our ethos has always been to offer equal space to all exhibiting publishers, whether small or large, from pamphlets to anthologies, in all styles of writing, in order to give the public a chance to explore everything that contemporary poetry publishing has to offer, all under one roof. We hope this almanac will help continue to make this happen.

This year, unlike in recent years, the Free Verse: Poetry Book Fair has been run without Arts Council funding. Although immensely grateful to them for previous grants, we were wary of expanding more than we'd ever reasonably be able to sustain ourselves, and so decided to try and make the Fair self-sustaining instead. We ran a wonderful competition to find love poems to display around the venue at this year's event (and also to be heard, at a short reading there) – we thought asking people to be creative was the best way to ask for their support. And, of course, we've also put this book together, building on and extending the publisher guides we've produced for previous Fairs. We hope you'll agree that it's a useful guide to the year in UK poetry publishing and, if so, that you'll tell other people about it.

We hope you enjoy this almanac, whether you are an aspiring or established poet, publisher or poetry reader. We hope it will open up the world of contemporary poetry and show you where delights are lurking, joining all the publishers together so you can see the wonderful, various world which they are all creating for us and which, of course, it is our pleasure to invest in.

Free Verse: Poetry Book Fair | www.poetrybookfair.com

What Excites Poetry Publishers?

Chrissy Williams

When contacting the 190 presses and organisations featured in this almanac, we took the opportunity to ask them which poetry books and publishers have excited them most over the past year.

There were a few publishers who were mentioned multiple times. These include the long-established book publishers Bloodaxe Books, Carcanet Press, Enitharmon, Reality Street and Shearsman, as well as the more (relatively speaking) recently established Burning Eye Books, CB editions, Eyewear Publishing, Happen*Stance* Press, Indigo Dreams Publishing and Valley Press. There were also multiple shout-outs to more experimental presses Shit Valley, Test Centre and zimZalla. The three publishers that were mentioned the most, however, were The Emma Press, Nine Arches Press and Penned in the Margins.

There were also many nods to other publishers, including Beautiful Dragons, Blart Books, Corbel Stone Press, If A Leaf Falls Press, Offa's Press, Tapsalteerie and Sine Wave Peak. This is only a handful though, and we encourage you to investigate any the unfamiliar names you find in this almanac.

Asking publishers which poetry book excited them most this year so far was wonderful – the only caveat was that it should not be one of their own. What's clear that everyone is being excited by an excitingly different number of books, which is exactly as it should be. 'The most exciting' does not mean 'the most new', nor does it mean it was published this year at all. The spread was so broad we thought we should reproduce it here in full, in the hope that it might offer a useful snapshot of excitement, without limitation by publication date, from the people whose job it is to read more book manuscripts each year than anyone else in the country.

There were a handful of this year's books which were recommended so many times they deserve special mention: *Cain* by Luke Kennard (Penned in the Margins), *Say Something Back* by Denise Riley (Picador), *Measures of Expatriation* by Vahni Capildeo (Carcanet) and *Falling Awake* by Alice Oswald (Cape Poetry). I notice all of these are also mentioned in John Clegg's essay, as well as (apart from *Cain*) being on this year's Forward Prize shortlists. Whatever can it all mean, I wonder?

Anyway. Please enjoy this list:

A Handbook for the Afterlife, Polly Clark (Templar, 2015)
Alive Alive O, Greta Stoddart (Bloodaxe Books, 2015)
An Anatomy of Melancholy, Tom Jenks (Sad Press, 2016)
[any translation of Dante] (n/a)
Bill Griffiths: Collected Poems Volume 3 (Reality Street, 2016)
Black Country, Liz Berry (Chatto & Windus, 2014)
Brother, Matthew & Michael Dickman (Faber & Faber, 2016)
Cain, Luke Kennard (Penned in the Margins, 2016)
Can I Borrow a Feeling? Anthology inspired by The Simpsons (Clinic, 2015)
Centres of Cataclysm: Celebrating 50 Years of Modern Poetry in Translation (Bloodaxe Books, 2016)
Chan, Hannah Lowe (Bloodaxe Books, 2016)
Citizen: An American Lyric, Claudia Rankine (Penguin Books, 2015)
Communing, Ben Banyard (Indigo Dreams, 2016)
Considering the Women, Choman Hardi (Bloodaxe Books, 2015)
Datableed (online poetry magazine – www.datableedzine.com)

Deerhart, Yvonne Reddick (Knives, Forks & Spoons Press, 2016)
Disinformation, Frances Leviston (Picador, 2015)
Dissolve to LA, James Trevelyan (The Emma Press, 2016)
Envies The Birds, Angelina D'Roza (Longbarrow Press, 2016)
Exotica Suite & Other Fictions, Wayne Burrows (Shoestring Press, 2015)
Falling Awake, Alice Oswald (Cape Poetry, 2016)
Fugitive Colours, Liz Lochhead (Birlinn, 2016)
Go to reception and ask for sara in red felt tip, Holly Pester (Book Works, 2015)
Gravity as a Consequence of Shape, Allen Fisher (Reality Street, 2016)
Hardly War, Don Mee Choi (Wave Books (USA), 2016)
Jutland, Selima Hill (Bloodaxe Books, 2015)
Lampshades and Glass Rivers, SA Leavesley (Lamplight Press, 2016)
Leasungspell, Bob Beagrie (Smokestack Books, 2016)
Letter From a Young Poet, Hyam Plutzik (Watkinson / Trinity College / Books and Books Press (USA), 2016)
Letters Against the Firmament, Sean Bonney (Enitharmon Books, 2015)
Long Shadows, Vuyelwa Carlin (Poetry Salzburg Press, 2016)
Loop of Jade, Sarah Howe (Chatto & Windus, 2015)
Love Songs of Carbon, Philip Gross (Bloodaxe Books, 2015)
Map: Collected and Last Poems, Wisława Szymborska (Houghton Mifflin, 2015)
Meanwhile, Trees, Mark Waldron (Bloodaxe Books, 2016)
Measures of Expatriation, Vahni Capildeo (Carcanet Press, 2016)
Meridian, Nancy Gaffield (Oystercatcher Press, 2016)
Milk and Honey, Rupi Kaur (Andrews McMeel Publishing, 2015)
My Dear Watson, The Very Elements of Poetry (anthology) (Beautiful Dragons Press, 2016)
My Family and Other Superheroes, Jonathan Edwards (Seren, 2014)
Night Sky with Exit Wounds, Ocean Vuong (Copper Canyon Press (USA), 2016)
Nothing Here is Wild, Everything is Open, Tania Hershman (Southword Editions (Republic of Ireland), 2016)

Owersettin, AC Clarke, Maggie Rabatski and Sheila Templeton (Tapsalteerie, 2016)
physical, Andrew McMillan (Cape Poetry, 2015)
Ramayana, Daljit Nagra (Faber & Faber, 2013)
Real South Bank, Chris McCabe (Seren, 2016)
Rumi (Everyman's Library Pocket Poets, 2006)
from 'Salt', David Harsent (*Poetry London* (magazine), 2015)
Sakura Park, Rachel Wetzsteon (Persea Books (USA), 2006)
Say Something Back, Denise Riley (Picador, 2016)
Serious Justice, Jen Calleja (Test Centre, 2016)
Several Deer, Adam Crothers (Carcanet Press, 2016)
Skin Diary, Abegail Morley (Nine Arches Press, 2016)
Slant Light, Sarah Westcott (Liverpool University Press (Pavilion Poetry), 2016)
Soft Troika, Lila Matsumoto (If A Leaf Falls Press, 2016)
Storysongs/Chantefables, Robert Desnos (trans. Timothy Ades) (Agenda Editions, 2014)
Strange Country, Kimberly Campanello (The Dreadful Press (Republic of Ireland), 2015)
The Art of Falling, Kim Moore (Seren, 2015)
The Art of Scratching, Shazea Quaraishi (Bloodaxe Books, 2015)
The Camphill Wren, James McGonigal (Red Squirrel Press, 2016)
The Collected Poems of Frank O'Hara (University of California Press (USA), 1995)
The Immigration Handbook, Caroline Smith (Seren, 2016)
The Nailmakers' Daughters (anthology) (Offa's Press, 2015)
The Poems of Basil Bunting (Faber & Faber, 2016)
The Poet, the Lion, Talking Pictures, El Farolito, a Wedding in St. Roch, the Big Box Store, the Warp in the Mirror, Spring, Midnights, Fire & All, CD Wright (Copper Canyon Press (USA), 2015)
The Quilted Multiverse, Jill Munro (Fair Acre Press, 2016)
The Rainbow Faults, Kate Wakeling (The Rialto, 2016)

The Stonegate Devil, Carole Bromley (smith | doorstop Books, 2015)
The Way The Crocodile Taught Me, Katrina Naomi (Seren, 2016)
TIN CAN WHITE GOWN, Alison Graham (PYRAMID Editions, 2016)
TRANS MANIFESTOS*, Verity Spott (Shit Valley, 2016)
Trouble, Alison Winch (The Emma Press, 2016)
Two Hundred Houses, Rachel Sills (Knives, Forks & Spoons Press, 2015)
Wait Till I'm Dead: Poems Uncollected, Allen Ginsberg (Penguin Modern Classics, 2016)
War of the Foxes, Richard Siken (Copper Canyon Press (USA), 2015)
Wound, Richard Scott (The Rialto, 2016)
[previously unread books], Anne Carson (n/a)

Which Publisher, and Are You Ready?

Helena Nelson, Excerpted from Chapter 3 of How (Not) To Get Your Poetry Published *(HappenStance Press, 2016)*

> *'... the literary publisher may occasionally be tempted by the commercial title in the hope of replenishing his bank balance and the commercial publisher may always be tempted by a literary title, since aspiring to prestige is a weed that grows everywhere.'*
>
> *—Roberto Calasso,* The Art of the Publisher *(Penguin Books, 2015, tr. Richard Dixon)*

Publishers are not all members of the same family. They're dramatically different from each other. The only thing they have in common is publications with poems in them.

Some poetry publishers have higher status than others. At the time of writing, the so-called 'big five' are Bloodaxe, Penguin Random House (includes Cape; Penguin Books; Chatto & Windus), Carcanet, Faber & Faber and Picador. Only two of these specialise mainly in poetry (Bloodaxe and Carcanet). The prestigious UK poetry prizes are usually (there are rare exceptions) won by collections from these publishing houses. This could mean they publish the best poetry of our era. This could mean they are the only publishers worth approaching, if fame and success are your goals.

But assume nothing. There are many kinds of 'success'. The world of poetry is far more full of opinions, blurb and hype than facts. The only true success for a poet is writing at least one good poem.

Getting work published is not the same as writing good poems.

Writing poetry and continuing to learn about that craft is the work of a lifetime. Finding the right publisher or editor can assist that process. Finding the wrong one means you're on your own. Or worse – praised where you should be challenged. In the meantime a lot of dodgy advice is floating about. Recently an aspiring poet I know was told by a worthy mentor: 'Send your manuscript to at least ten publishers at once'.

The key (to my mind) is not how many publishers you send to but which ones you choose to approach, and why. Most people hoping to have work published find their way to the current addresses of publishers via one route or another. Many can be found on more than one website, such as that of Southbank Centre Poetry Library, as well as inside library reference books such as *The Writers and Artists Yearbook*, or *The Writer's Handbook* (**Ed** – although the most comprehensive listing by far lies in the volume you hold in your hands right now].

So this is what some poets do next, first in your list of things not to do. They click on, or type out, the email address (often without even reading the information carefully) and send a message to the publisher. As Happen*Stance* editor, I had two such emails only last week (from separate poets). They read something like this:

> *Dear Editor*
>
> *I have a collection of poems I would like to get published. Please tell me something about your preferences so I know whether it is worth sending to you.*
>
> *Yours sincerely*
> *Doug Wright*

Dear Sir or Madam:

I am interested in publishing my collection of poems provisionally titled The Hearts and Minds of Oceans. Could you tell me something about what kind of poetry you usually prefer? Some of my poems have violent or sexual content that might not be to everyone's taste.

You will be able to read a selection of my poems at my website: www.AmazingAmanda.com. Please take a look and let me know if you are interested. Thank you for your time.

Amanda Aberystwyth-Perkins
Amy@AmazingAmanda.com

These emails were a waste of time for their authors. Why? Because all they've done is reveal ignorance and apparent laziness. The writers haven't bothered to find the name of the editor (in the age of the internet, this is child's play). And there's no point asking a publisher what he or she prefers. It simply shows you know nothing about their publishing record and current list of poets.

Worse still, the author of the second example has an extremely memorable name (though in this case fictional). So that means if Amanda Aberystwyth-Perkins makes another, more carefully prepared, approach in the future, she'll be remembered as Amazing Amanda who sent an email without finding the name of the editor or knowing anything about the imprint.

But I'm sure you're better prepared than this. You may even be looking for someone to take on your *second* book. You will need to present yourself to the publisher as a viable proposition. Are u in a position to do this? It's useful to do a swift self-appraisal your 'success' so far:

- List at least six paper magazines that have printed your work in the last three years.
- If you have publications already in print (books, pamphlets), note them down.
- If you have had poems in anthologies, list the books in which they appear, with publication dates.
- Does your work appear on the web? If so, where? List sites, including your own, if applicable.
- Have you won or been placed in any poetry competitions? If so, list your triumphs, with dates.

Right. That's a brief overview of your public self. I have asked you to list magazines that have published your work. I haven't asked you to consider how much kudos they carry. But it isn't rocket science to work out which are most prestigious. The top journals often *pay* authors for publication – I mean actual money. They're also costly to subscribe to and usually have some public funding.

Online, the most desirable ezines publish well-known poets, so look for names you recognise. Another way to work out which publications carry clout is to look inside the debut books of recent first collection prize-winners and see which magazines they acknowledge. It's likely they've been placing their poems judiciously. Watch and take note.

Now – more questions over the page to test your readiness:

- What are the names of the (poetry) editors of the following presses? Bloodaxe Books, Faber & Faber, Cinnamon, Carcanet, Picador, Liverpool University Press (Pavilion Poetry), Cape, Seren, Nine Arches, Indigo Dreams.

- List the names of five poetry pamphlet imprints (book publishers mentioned above are excluded from this list)?

- Name ten poetry collections (books or pamphlets) you've read in the last two years, and say who the publisher was for each one.

Okay. How did you get on? If you found it hard to answer these questions, I suggest there's some way to go before you can approach a publisher, and I haven't yet started on the research required. You need an informed understanding of who does what before you can enter the fray with a decent chance of success.

If you answered most of my questions fairly easily, well done. But it's about to get harder. Here's the bottom line: in order to get a collection of poetry published with a reputable publisher (like every other aspect of life there are exceptions) you must already have placed *individual* poems widely, in well-regarded outlets.

If you're looking for a book-length collection, it would be an advantage to have already published at least one pamphlet that was well reviewed and sold well. This would suggest you've already created at least a small readership. Some experience of public reading (again with some good feedback) would also be advantageous.

You don't have to have won any competitions, though it's nice if you have.

You don't need to be rich.

You don't need endorsements from well-known poets, especially not well-known poets who write endorsements for lots of people.

You don't have to have your own website.

But you do need to know your way around the world wide web. You do need to use email. You need to be able to say the word 'internet' without groaning.

But first, there's the issue of the magazines. Why do you need to get poems in magazines? Why can't they just go straight into a book? (**Ed** – to keep following this advice, you'll have to read on in the book... Details below!)

*Helena Nelson is the publisher at Happen*Stance *Press. This piece has been excerpted from her excellent book* How (Not) To Get Your Poetry Published, *available now from Happen*Stance.

A (Subjective) Introduction to Innovative Presses

SJ Fowler

Without doubt, the avant-garde, the modernist, the innovative – that which I would deem 'contemporary' rather than experimental – has undergone a renaissance in the UK over the last decade. Whether it's aligned to the increased connectivity of the internet, mindblowing as it is as a global, language-based cultural nervous system, or the world population doubling, or something less fundamental, I'm not sure. But there are more poets working in this tradition in the UK than is easily followed or fathomed.

This has been in no small part maintained and driven by a number of publishers, events, organisers and poets themselves. Below is an idiosyncratic, limited and subjective run down of a few you should check out, should you want to read poetry that reflects today, in all its adversarial complexity.

Publishers-wise, you can't go wrong following the exploits of Knives Forks and Spoons Press, Shearsman, Veer Books, Test Centre, If P Then Q, Blart Books, Stranger Press, Etruscan, Reality Street, West House Books, Very Small Kitchen, Barque, Information as Material, and certainly Penned in the Margins, Carcanet, Eyewear, CB editions, Enitharmon, Bloodaxe, Arc, Faber, Penguin also have innovative poets on their lists too.

For smaller publications, chapbooks, pamphlets and limited editions, aside from the healthy zine-making scene, there are dozens of open submission presses all over the islands – worth checking out Oystercatcher, Red Ceilings, zimZalla, Pyramid Editions, Department Press, Moot Press, Crater, Four Fold, Sine Wave Peak.

Readings like Xing the Line, The The the, Shearsman Reading series, Praxis, The Blue Bus, The Enemies Project (all in London) plus The Other Room, which also runs the website www.otherroom.org (which I would say is an invaluable resource), Peter Barlow's Cigarette (both in Manchester) Caesura (Edinburgh) Storm and Golden Sky (Liverpool), are some of many events happening all over the UK. Along with the Other Room site, Peter Philpott's www.modernpoetry.org.uk is a great entry point.

These things are always in flux, driven by certain individuals, collectives and organisations that have decided to take control of the space in which poetry is read and heard, but hopefully this is a useful inroad, as a very rudimentary note, to a world of brilliant poetry being made in the UK at the moment.

SJ *Fowler is a poet, artist and curator. His most recent collection* {Enthusiasm} *is published by Test Centre.*

On Publishing Spoken Word Poetry

Clive Birnie

Burning Eye Books has been going since 2012, and specialises in promoting spoken word artists. What first drew you to this area of publishing?

The empty space that other poetry publishers had left for me to move into. I wanted to do something that would add something to the poetry scene and found myself sat in sold out theatre audiences for poets who were unpublished and unlikely to be published. It was a classic market gap. There was clearly demand for the poetry as the poets were filling rooms with paying customers. I saw creating Burning Eye as being similar to starting an indie record label to serve a niche music scene.

What are the benefits to spoken word artists of having their work published in book form?

Money and credibility. The driving purpose of Burning Eye is to assist poets in making more money from their work to enable them to live from their art and our publishing deal is structured to assist that. Credibility wise Burning Eye is established enough now to mean something and our poets tell me being published by Burning Eye helps them get booked at bigger, better paying events.

Is it okay to read a book by an artist if you haven't already seen them live (and therefore don't already know their voice / delivery etc)?

Definitely, like any other poetry though you only really know how it sounded in the mind of the writer when you hear the poet read / perform. I cannot read 'At Roane Head' without hearing Robin Robertson's growl echoing in my head. Seeing a live performance enhances our understanding of any poetry but good poetry of all kinds will hold its own if encountered only on the page.

Do you see a book as a complete work, or just one aspect of the work itself (e.g. like publishing a book of song lyrics, without the music)?

I sometimes say the book is to the performance what the studio album is to the live gig. Two versions of the same thing but many people will see the book / studio version as the definitive version.

You do books, and also books for YouTube – could you talk a bit about the different formats you publish in and why you've chosen them? Is it different for each artist you work with?

The books for YouTube is a specific collaboration with the illustrator / film maker Guy Larsen. I don't necessarily see it as something we would extend. Otherwise the approach has become a standard process (it has to be to enable the publication of twenty titles a year) although we occasionally try out different ideas – Geoff Allnut and Annabel Munn's Dr Seuss parody *The Twat in the Flat* for instance which is a full colour and illustrated in the style of the original. We have produced a few full colour illustrated books now, Hollie McNish's *Cherry Pie* and Rebecca Tantony's *Talk You Round Till Dusk* being standouts. Rebecca's book is beautiful on every level and the illustrations by the artist Anna Higgie are stunning. Both were pitched to me as finished concepts and Rebecca and Hollie had creative control over (almost) every aspect of the books.

What are the main challenges involved in bringing work created for performance onto the page?

Not to mess with work that has been honed out loud and try to put it down on paper even if that sometimes means leaving some raw and rough edges in place.

Which spoken word artists are you most excited about at the moment?

Agnes Török whose book *Happiness is an Art Form* was out in August – poetry as therapy – one of the best books I have worked on. The three poets we are showcasing at Free Verse, Laurie Bolger, Emily Harrison and Jemima Foxtrot and the one who couldn't make it to the fair, Sara Hirsch. Vanessa Kisuule has a new book in progress which I hope to have out during 2017. I have a feeling that is going to be something significant. Vanessa is a stand out artist for me. The thought process she applies. The way she deliberately goes out and takes on challenging new experiences and then feeds that method-actor-style back into her creative process is astonishing. Also Salena Godden is on fire at the moment. Some recent performances have been career bests and that is saying something.

Clive Birnie is the publisher at Burning Eye Books.

On Selling Poetry

John Clegg

As this is supposed to be an Almanac (and as I am writing this on the till computer and have easy access to our databases) I will try and incorporate as many facts, figures, and omens as possible.

I work for the LRB Bookshop in Bury Place (one of the cuts between High Holborn and Great Russell Street), and poetry is our bestselling category after fiction. (We sell about three times as much fiction as poetry. Poetry amounts to about 10% of our total sales.) I think we have one of the best selections in the country; we certainly have an unusually large selection. (Six thousand titles, as of the 28th July.) Over the last year our poetry sales have increased by about 10%. Whether this is part of a nationwide trend, you had better ask the publishers – I am quietly optimistic. Books on the uneasy margin between poetry and prose (like Maggie Nelson's *Bluets*, or Claudia Rankine's *Citizen*) have done a lot to 'normalise' poetry as a genre – or, rather, to make it less a genre, more a 'kind of writing'. (I know this is not much of a distinction. But: we get a lot of customers who don't want any sci-fi novels, far fewer who don't want any first-person novels. Works like *Bluets* have been helping to move poetry from the first category into the second.)

Another reason to be cheerful is that it's a vintage year for poetry. Denise Riley's *Say Something Back*, Vahni Capildeo's *Measures of Expatriation*, Alice Oswald's *Falling Awake* and Luke Kennard's *Cain* are all astonishing collections. But our increase doesn't seem to be caused by a few particular titles doing very well – rather it's across the board.

A few fairly unremarked changes are likely to have a substantial effect on poetry bookselling over the next few years:

- Under James Daunt, Waterstones has successfully reversed a lot of the disastrous business practices brought in by former director and schlub Gerry Johnson. This has allowed individual stores more leeway in their choice of where to specialise, and quite a few Waterstones stores have excellent poetry sections at the moment.

- Book distribution is of interest to literally no one apart from booksellers, so I'll keep this short. Inpress, an Arts Council-funded umbrella group representing a lot of small publishers, are moving distribution from Central to NBN. This will make it (slightly) easier for (most) bookshops to order small-press poetry titles.

- A small procedural change in the TS Eliot Prize rules means that Poetry Book Society Choices are no longer automatically nominated for the prize. This suits booksellers down to the ground, because when a PBS Choice ends up winning the boost in sales is smaller (since PBS members have already been sent the book).

- Print-on-demand technology continues to improve, and is becoming more incorporated into supply chains. Backlist titles are more available than they were (some of the interesting Salt backlist, for instance, has become available again).

Finally, as promised, an omen, which I heard as true on good authority:

The Waterstones in Islington received in their delivery two copies of the NYRB reissue of JH Prynne's *The White Stones*, which they had not ordered and which did not appear on the invoice. Nevertheless they were booked into stock. By the end of the day, both had sold, and so the manager arranged for the title to be reordered. The next day, both the new copies had sold, and it went on doing a steady two a day, which caused some consternation since nobody remembered it ever passing through the tills. Piqued by curiosity, the manager investigated the book one morning, opening it on the poem called 'A Figure of Mercy, of Speech':

> On the hilt of fortune: so that he
> asks the time and it's grey, with
> almost solemn insistence. Yes it is…

As he cycled home the words seemed to reverberate through his spokes. And beneath them, a certain undertone. As he lay on the brink of sleep, the poetry faded and the undertone rose: a thousand voices, chanting as one, the syllables becoming just perceptible, 'Come aboard the Moloch, come aboard the Moloch'. If a car alarm two streets away hadn't gone off at that moment and woken him up, it's very unsure where he would be today. As it is, the store's poetry section is thriving; but if a customer ever asks him the time, he turns pale, mumbles something non-commital, and hurries off to do some shelving. As must I.

John Clegg works at the LRB Bookshop. His most recent collection of poems, Holy Toledo!, *is published by Carcanet Press.*

Poetry and Race

Abridged transcript of an event at the 2015 Poetry Book Fair with Malika Booker, Hannah Lowe, Hannah Silva and Nii Parkes.

MALIKA BOOKER: "I'm going to start off by talking about The Complete Works programme. There was an initiative by the Arts Council to have an investigation into the state of publishing, and it found that less than 1% of all poetry books being published in the UK were by BAME poets. You can read that Free Verse report online. It's very comprehensive and it came out in 2005. As a result, Bernardine Evaristo started an initiative called The Complete Works which was designed to address that.

The poets were saying they had no access to networks, to the literary publishing network. So The Complete Works decided that it would be a development initiative, linking all of us (I was one of the ten poets who were on the first programme) with an establishment poet. My poet was WN Herbert. So, the aim was to develop the writing, but also to introduce us to the publishers. And that was a wonderful experience. It was the first time for a lot of us that our writing was seen as literary, was seen as important, and was talked about on its merit as writing. And as a result of that, the anthology *Ten* was published, which did really really well. They published a selection of the poets on the scheme, but also added introductions by their mentors, and those essays were really great in enabling people to see the work.

In an issue of *Poetry Review* that came out in 2012, Daljit Nagra talks about being one of the editors on The Complete Works, and he talks about the fact that he's been educated in a completely British establishment, so some of the challenges of working on The Complete Works involved 'taste'. And so the word 'taste' came on the table – something that hadn't been talked about before.

For example, Mir Mahfuz Ali's and my work was very visceral and really went for the emotional jugular – Daljit's response as an editor was to try and pull that back, because he comes from a space where it's about subtlety, it's about hinting. Editors who are editing and trying to be open to other communities need to think about their taste, because maybe when we're talking about quality of work, we're talking about challenges that come up in terms of taste.

So we come on to The Complete Works II. The publishing of poets of colour has moved to 10%, with twenty poets being developed, and so the landscape is changing, but I think we also need to look at what's happening in terms of the collections being reviewed.

If collections are not reviewed, then they're not opened out to a reading by the public. So we need to look at who is reviewing the books, as well as looking at prizes, and changing how we do prizes; I think we need to think about diversity in terms of judging, and diversity in terms of reviewing. Because now we have a phenomenon where books are coming out, and they're not being reviewed. And so if they're not being picked up by the *Poetry Review*, by *Poetry London*, by all the spaces where people look to tell them what's the latest book, that's problematic.

I'm going to finish by saying there's something problematic when every time we see the judging, the judges, the books that have been shortlisted – we have Penned in the Margins, we have Peepal Tree, we have so many different publishers – but if you look at the judging panels, you will think that it's only Carcanet, Bloodaxe and Faber that publish books and are purveyors of poetry, and of quality poetry. So I think there is a big discussion to be had."

HANNAH LOWE: "I'd like to talk quite differently to Malika, about my own personal dialogue with poetry as it relates to race, and I kind of feel like I might have to get on the psychologist's couch now, for some of the things I'm going to say about my own journey through poetry. *Chick*, which was my collection from 2013, was the first place I ever made a tentative claim on any other identity than the one you would assume me to have through looking at me; it was the first place I really wrote about the fact that my dad was Jamaican. He was half black Jamaican and half Chinese, and I'll talk a little bit about his history, to explain to you why poetry became so important to me.

He was born really in poverty in the Caribbean in 1925, he came to Britain in 1947, and worked his whole life as a gambler and card sharp, a very marginalised and unstable existence really, and when he died – he got ill when I was in my late teens and he died when I was 22 – I felt an enormous amount of grief that I had never really asked him about his life. We didn't talk a lot, he suppressed a lot, I never really knew his story, and I felt that with his death my only connection to that heritage was severed. How would anyone know that I was that, if he wasn't there to prove it, I suppose.

And so it was many years later that I began to write poetry, and by that time it was almost as though I couldn't sit on it any longer, even at university I was always drawn towards studying black women's writing and then after university I did an MA in refugee studies. It was like d'uh, why are you interested in this stuff? I never made those connections. And when I wrote *Chick* I never set out to claim a mixed-race identity or be a spokesperson for multiculturalism, I just wanted to write about mine and his relationship I suppose. And my unusual upbringing – I guess I thought it was important to begin to complicate some of the ideas that people hold about race. Not to be glib about this at all – the fact that I come from a mixed race background and 300 years ago on plantations in the Caribbean or in the deep south of America, there were people that looked like me that would have been slaves. You will have heard these sorts of ideas, to do with the particular concept of 'passing', so I started really wanting to probe those ideas, but it was a great surprise to me when *Chick* was accepted, and reviewed in magazines like *The Voice*. And I began to be asked to be involved in black writing, and I still question myself about how much I can contribute to those events or what my place is. I suppose it's a deep anxiety about feeling that I've got no claim to a shared identity with them, and that mainly is because of racism of course, which is not something that has been my experience, because I pass for something else by and large.

So what I would say about poetry specifically is that because of the acceptance that I've had – and it wasn't just in poetry, but also for research trips I was able to take, that came after *Chick*, to the Caribbean for example – I found that voice seemed to be valid in some of these debates about race, which certainly encouraged me to carry on writing about some of these issues and perhaps become bolder in my writing. So for example my pamphlet *Ormonde*, is all about the fact that my dad came on a boat before the Windrush, an unknown ship called the Ormonde. And my second collection of poetry (*Chan*) is very engaged with writing about – and also mimetically and formally trying to replicate – some of these ideas and confusions about mixed raceness.

I still feel kind of that confusion about the whole thing, so for example next week I've been asked to do an Arts Council event, to talk to black and minority ethnic writers, about how to get funding, and I wonder how I will proceed in that environment.

I certainly know that some of the organisations I've worked with have ticked the BAME box when I'm involved in their work, and I suppose I guess that is right, but it's still something that slightly haunts me. In a way what I'm trying to get at is that poetry is a mission to explore an identity that is otherwise suppressed. And so I'm very grateful to the poetry community, and of course I'm pleased that I've been able to make an inroad there."

HANNAH SILVA: "I'm doing a PhD on Black British Poetry in Performance. It's actually a PhD that was advertised by the British Library and Stirling University. I saw the title and I saw the description of the PhD and I only glanced at it initially as I've not got a background in post-colonial literature, and I hadn't spent much time considering black Britishness. Obviously I'm white. I can't speak from a black British experience. But I found myself writing a list of poets that could be studied within that PhD. It was a very very long list and included a number of poets that I've shared the stage with, who have been really important to me over the years, and got excited about the project. During my interview for it I noted the fact to my interviewers that we were in a room full of white people (there were about five of us in that room). I said, 'Is this a problem? I notice this – is this is a problem?' And they turned the question back on me and said, 'Do you think this is a problem?', and I said 'yes!'.

But then I said that this is indicative of a wider problem within academia – implying that it was not their fault personally – I wanted the opportunity. But in fact I suspect that the only way of changing the wider problem is to not keep giving white students like me this kind of opportunity. But I don't know who else interviewed and of course I'm delighted to be doing this, I love doing the research and feel a lot of responsibility to do it well.

I spent the first year being a bit uncomfortable, thinking and reading about black Britishness, feeling that as a white person, and white people have always historically been the definers, that I didn't want to do that, I didn't want to be in a position of defining. And I didn't want to create a kind of category, 'This is black British poetry', not only because I'm a white researcher but also because I have a difficulty with categories anyway – they exclude, and it seemed to me that the poets that I was most interested in were the ones that didn't fit easily into labels and categories (in fact no one does). And so I got more comfortable with being uncomfortable, but that's a problem also, that throughout academia there are a lot of white researchers who are comfortable with being uncomfortable.

After that period of discomfort I realised that what I can bring to the project is close analysis of performance. So Malika mentioned the Free Verse report, and one of the things that that report identified was that publishing, getting published in print, was the big barrier to get through. There are a lot of poets working in performance; performance is a very diverse area within the poetry scene. The only diverse area, really. But the report identified this as partly the problem – that a black or Asian writer is assumed to be a performance poet based on their skin colour. And that is a problem because performance poetry was seen as lesser, and there is still that perception, I think. So one way of approaching this problem is to give more opportunities to support publication which is what has been done by the Complete Works programme, but another way I think is to raise performance, is to find a critical vocabulary for talking about performance which is equal to the kind of critical vocabulary that's applied to poetry on the page. To find a place within academia to talk about performance.

An interesting thing was said last year by Bernardine Evaristo at the launch of the second anthology of the Complete Works programme: she said that this might be controversial, but performance poetry is a separate genre. Some of the poets in that anthology are brilliant performers and have established themselves through performance. So what does it mean if their performance work is a separate genre? She wasn't actually referring to *their* work in performance, but how do we separate 'performance poets' from 'poets'? And is that at all useful? I can understand the desire to do so if performance poetry is seen as lesser, but I'm not sure that's a useful approach. So yes, you can say that these poets are great performers of their work, but they're not performance poets – but then, who is a performance poet? And can that really be separate from poetry? I don't think it can, but I think we need to talk more critically about poetry in performance, and see the layers of performance such as use of voice and the body and all the choices made during delivery as part of poetry, as an active part of 'writing'.

It's also worth mentioning that even when discussing poetry in performance, there's always the page too, and an interaction with the poem on the page (even when poets recite rather than read). But the page version of the poem is not *the* version. There are multiple versions."

NII PARKES: "I grew up in Ghana, with a different reality where some of these kinds of entitlements and gatekeepers that are relating to race don't exist. When I wrote it was valid, of course it was valid, and that's what I knew. So when I came here and started going to poetry events and listening to poets and reading poetry, I was able to look at it dispassionately, and actually a lot of what we're talking about in terms of race is really about entitlement and humility. I mean, it's got nothing to do with race at all, and that's what has been used time and again to kind of... It's agenda setting. Anyone who's done communications science will know about these things.

So I'll give you a simple example. I run a small press. I'm talking from the perspective of poets or writers. If someone sends a manuscript to me, and within three years I haven't gotten round to publishing it, they will throw a tantrum. If Faber & Faber said we're going to publish that manuscript, and they waited ten years, they'd still be waiting, without complaining. So that's the kind of level of perception that you have to be aware of within the industry. And then you have to think about the framing: what's the agenda, what's really the agenda – and it's stopping certain people from getting published, and allowing certain people to be published, and then you realise that's the way in which poetry has developed, really in this country. The voice comes first. So there should be no debate about whether poetry isn't a form, or whether the page is superior, because without the voice, the writing wouldn't have come in the first place. And then the theory comes after the writing – of what kind of curating you need in the writing.

And what's happened, essentially, is that when poetry started being written it was a kind of upper-class pastime. It was written, it was analysed in the universities – there were ways developed of reading poems which had nothing to do with people who didn't work in that environment. So, the first actual division that happened in poetry was certain people of certain classes weren't allowed in: 'As a commoner, you can't publish'; 'That's not poetry'; 'It's not referring to Greek gods'... And then it became a gender thing: 'It's too emotional'; 'We can't figure this out'; 'We can't publish that'. And then it became a continent thing: 'Oh the Americans, they're so crass'. Honestly, if you look at the history of poetry, this is happening time and again, until it comes to the most obvious difference, race.

So it's important to think about these things outside of this [race]. What I've done as an editor, always, is to say, 'I'm not going to tell you this is wrong, I'm going to ask you why you've done it. And if you can't explain it, then we'll talk about how it might be corrected.' And this is how come I've been lucky to publish so many great poets, because a lot of other people have said to them, 'I don't understand this, this is irrelevant to what I know, it doesn't fall within some structure, it's not the next Seamus Heaney'. And so they were turned back.

Talking about the first Complete Works programme – five of those poets had been published by me already, so that's how far behind the zeitgeist the establishment is. Because we found that as publishers we were selling more than your Fabers et cetera by acknowledging that there's a reading public that doesn't have to have gone to Oxford or Cambridge – that we can sell directly to them. If you don't want to stock us in stores, we will go out and do performances, and people will buy those books. And so every single one of these poets was outselling some of these names that you see in the news all the time.

It's about understanding that this is about people's authority. Because the publishers are saying to you, 'You can't get this', which is an insult really, and they don't even give you the chance to not get it. They're saying, 'We're not going to publish this because we don't get it. And so *they* won't get it.' Which is nonsense, because actually the people who work in academia, who work at those levels, are the minority. You can't put the whole country into Oxford or Cambridge, right? So what's happening essentially is that if you allow all these brilliant voices to come up, with all their different shades and colours – what happens is that your professor of poetry in Cambridge can't rely on stuff he's known for 50 years. It means he has to keep digging, it means he has to keep working. Now, if electricians have to do that, why shouldn't professors of poetry? Electricians have to do that, plumbers have to do that, gas workers have to do that – they're recertifying all the time. In academia they don't want to do that. And editors don't want to learn new things. It [is a system that] doesn't work. And that's really the level at which we should be looking at this. Even as readers. We should be complaining to these publishers, to people in academia. If you go and someone's teaching you, if you're a student of poetry, and you ask them, 'have you heard of Roger Robinson?' and they say 'no'... 'God damn, you should read them! So we can talk about it next week!' And that's where we should be going from. I mean, yes; race is the most obvious thing, but it's bigger than that, and that's what I think we need to focus on."

This panel was put together by Malika Booker for the 2015 Free Verse: Poetry Book Fair. It has been transcribed and edited for length.

Malika Booker is a writer, poet, multi-disciplinary artist coach and teacher. Her collection Pepper Seed *is available from Peepal Tree Press. Hannah Lowe is a poet and tutor. Her most recent collection* Chan *is available from Bloodaxe Books. Hannah Silva is a poet, playwright and performer. Her collection* Forms of Protest *is available from Penned in the Margins. Nii Parkes is a poet and novelist, and is the publisher at Flipped Eye Publishing. His collection* The Makings of You *is available from Peepal Tree Press.*

Poetry from 2016

as selected by the publishers

How long it takes to walk without sound

By the time you open your eyes—
that's how long it takes for dusk
to deplete the walls, to hear the cat
grow fat, as ink from artificial lashes

streams like seconds—the kiss
of Judas, not to the cheek, but to silence—
time sniffs through corners and sends out
its pit-bulls while sleep wears away—

the ozone of serenity has grown thin,
and blinders—cast-iron moths—
begin to flap until they surrender
and break off to one side.

You open your eyes—December dark.
The meditating cat grows, and likewise
what you betray—what you have,
what you pursue, what you protect.

You open your eyes—the footprints
of sleep, still breathing, dry like rain.
To embrace without touching—
I walk silently through the lilacs.

Ilzė Butkutė, trans. from the Lithuanian by Rimas Uzgiris
Caravan Lullabies, A Midsummer Night's Press

The Old Order

I don't remember how
the conversation got round to God,
but suddenly my father
was strumphing at the end of the table,
everyone else zip-lipped.

It was like the time I snorted
when he said the sun never set
on the British Empire.
He stood up. I beat a hasty retreat,
my handkerchief a white flag.

When his arguments fell on deaf ears
he often raised his hand if not his game.
But anyway, I see it now,
now he's gone,
and the Empire's gone, and God, even God,

what it must have been like for him,
raised in that fortress of certainties,
to see it breached by his own daughter,
dammit, his daughter,
telling him what was what.

Ann Alexander
Old Things, from the Acumen archive

What the Burglar Took

That night it was nothing.
Cinematic, he'd slid
under the kitchen window,
swerved an old veined saucer,
rocked the vintage cactus,
slippered his way across tiles
on a moulting rug
that still smelt of your last dog
and made you wheeze.

After that threshold no sign,
yet you felt him in every omission -
the carriage clock that paced him
but never chimed, silver fish
partying by moonlight who'd fled
into covens of dust, slivers
of street-lamp that laid a grid
from back to front room
where shadows failed to creak.

His exit, another window,
half open in the study.
The room was rigid with night,
The Great Bear
encrypted in the cushions.
You touched frost on the inside,
took to spying on your house,
heard whispers in the heating kettle
morse in the water-pipes.

Rosalind Hudis
Agenda, 2016 , Agenda Poetry

Psalms of Devotion 1

Between our torn, upset lips even the
spinning, straining words are banished,
rounding into kisses here between the
ornate eyelashes in our interlocked
admiring eyes and they die without
making a sound; what they are born
on to is a sumptuous gift, a hymnal
vision and the winged, clapping embrace of
yellow orioles on a wise kiss's broad trunk.

Miklós Radnóti, trans. from the Hungarian by Mark Somos
Snow lit rev, 4, Spring 2016, Allardyce, Barnett, Publishers

XX

egg custards make impractical train food
however this has to be preferable
to hanging around at home even with
fresh turbot in the fridge or stuck alone
in some hipster bar with no smokes to bum
I love you fading on the love heart
and a dirty burger to go. Go where?
You don't want me snivelling in the face
of all known germs including the good ones:
I was shouting I'm burning I'm burning
but like the Wichita Lineman I'm still
on the line just discernible under
the pile-up of shadows contemplating
an existentialist haircut right now.

Anthony Mellors
Confessional Sonnets, Aquifer Books

Acrostic Twenty-One

For a Peruvian child: 'To Margarita Ulloa Elías'

Though I'm absolutely an
Out-of-your-area man,
Margarita, I pursue
A conference with you
Revealing my hesitancies:
Giving (if I apply
Absence profitably)
Rhymes whose assonances
Imitate my aspiring,
Tough, tricky and tiring,
Audaciously loyal - to you.
Unusual wishes of this
Lass far away in Peru -
Look at her caprices,
Odd and well-known to you:
A line that ends with a u...
Emending, with one eye shut, she's
Lightened a poet's flat feet,
Imposing on him (how neat!)
Acrostics as his crutches. –
So I wonder, will this do?

Alfonso Reyes, trans. from the Mexican by Timothy Adès

Acumen, c/o Assorted Translations

& with thanks to Fondo de Cultura Económica

Only Listen

Imagine what might happen
if you shut your mouth and listened:

you might fall into a thousand
pieces of light

each irradiated
with birdsong and blue sky

each of them speaking
your original name.

In all your senses –
hearing, tasting,
touching, smelling, and sensing –
fill them with listening

and you will find yourself again.

*

And when you have become your listening
your breath will heal you of all misgiving

and all the tightness you have held
all over your body and being

will become a babbling stream of healing,
caressing and soothing, sustaining every cell …

and you will be the one you always were within,
who silently lives underneath everything.

*

And if you listen, high above the sound of the water
in the sun-dappled beech trees like a church built
all around the birdsong – you may hear

a flute: dipping, and gliding, and soaring
in and out of the stillness of a dream …

And long after the girl who played the flute has gone
you will hear, or imagine you hear, her song …

half-heard between the leaf-breeze and the stream
where it has become your listening.

Jay Ramsay
Places of Truth: Journeys into Sacred Wilderness,
Awen Publications

II

Oops & Whoops

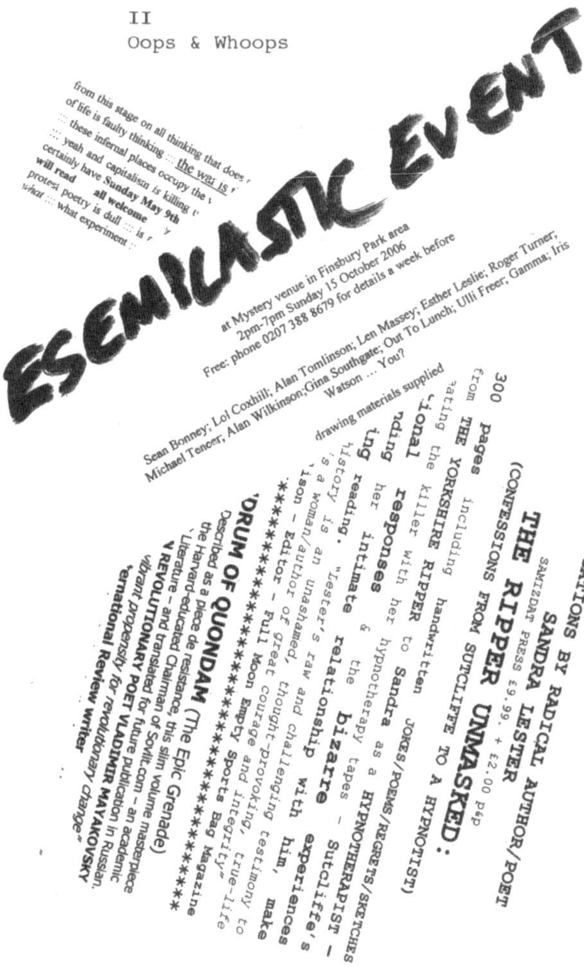

MJ Weller

Three Piece Bathing Suit, Blart Books

Yes I admit that I have ate

that once cool and heavy egg that would
one day have hatched a clever goose of gold.

I cooked it in a pan until it smelted from a hard
into a runny yolk,

and then I promptly drank the molten yellow,
gulped it down and felt it start to burn away

my tongue and gums and teeth whose residue
then blew away as smoke. I felt it coursing down

my roasting throat, through the squiggle
of my blistered viscera,

all the way beyond my screaming shitter
from which it oozed and swarmed and spread

wet metal excrement about my seared balls
and buttocks, before it slowly made to thicken.

And once I'd died of pain, then some time
afterwards I ate away my flesh and bone:

I sank my corpse in acid till no bit of it remained
but just this shiny winding cast, this meandered

single golden sprue that rises from its golden stand,
and displayed like this so well describes a fool.

Mark Waldron
Meanwhile, Trees, Bloodaxe Books

biscuit crumb
delicious
as stolen love

Ilyana Stoyanova
Blithe Spirit 26.1, British Haiku Society

this game of staring
the ginger cat next door
always wins

David Cobb
Blithe Spirit 26.2, British Haiku Society

a lifetime
overcoming gravity –
still it gets me down

David Bingham
Blithe Spirit 26.3, British Haiku Society

I Can't Sleep 'Cause My Bed's on Fire

I turn to a nurse and say,
'If there's one place you can't be embarrassed about your dance moves,
it's in a psych ward.'
I had joked earlier, sat down plastic next to Danny.
'What you get?'
'Double vodka Coke.'
We find courage
thumbing the ridges of the vending machine cup.
Tonight, Friday night, is a game of musical paper plates.
It's much harder to drag someone up to the dance floor
without physical contact
but slowly others join us
as if someone held up a huge cardboard sign
telling them they were allowed to.
Danny, arm in sling, does his best to show off and to me
it looks like the first time he has ever danced.
I watch from the fence,
his pupils sink,
as if with a hard enough wish
he could turn water into wine.

Emily Harrison
I Can't Sleep 'Cause My Bed's on Fire, Burning Eye Books

[untitled]

Red flicker through the trees. The last minibus
leaves from the station, heading for the tops
full of ghosts, ghosts with notebooks, ancestors
from Halifax: farmers, publicans, clerks, looking
for me, wanting me back in the peace and jubilee
of diurnal normality. But they have caught
the wrong bus and will be delivered into nothing,
the nothing of death they came from, and came here
to welcome me to. Passing the abandoned chapel
they start singing hymns, and will soon begin to fade.
Down here another train rolls in and the dark river
splashes past on the stones of demolished mills, let go of me.

Peter Riley
Pennine Tales, Calder Valley Poetry

Dirt

I want the dust beneath the fridge to hold the DNA
of generations. I want to lift the delicate carcass
of an insect from the carpet. I want to sit by the window
and watch water in the gutter and when I pull back the
sheets I want them dirty. I want the dirt on my hands.
I want it wet because there's rain and I've trucked
through mud to get here. I want saliva and spit and I
want that part of your mind. To celebrate it. To act it out.
There's dignity there. Lay yourself open. We'll both
blossom. If you want me to call you a whore, I'll do it.
Stand in the muck with me. Live amongst the flowers.

William Letford
Dirt, Carcanet Press

In Memory Of Amy Winehouse

Hot weather in London quickly feels bizarrely
natural. It was my first evening at the
swanky flat near Oxford Street which my then new
girlfriend was renting. The soft air
was hazy or even slightly heavy with happiness
as we walked round the neighbourhood. We
got together for a while and then broke up,
and got back together and later broke up completely. But
all of this was some time ago now. At the top
of the street amongst drifts of late evening warmth,
we saw Amy Winehouse standing there with a cigarette.
She looked tiny and sumptuous and slightly lost at the edge of
a small group of softly talking friends. She
looked in fact to me like poetry summed up, so lavish
but at the same time so starkly factual. Her black
voice sat inside her and watched the future go
by with its warm hands full of shadows.

Patrick Mackie
The Further Adventures Of The Lives Of The Saints, CB editions

The Shed

not much more than a pile of driftwood
hammered together, a makeshift roof,
window, door

someone's been in here

but already the sand is blowing inside
and the sea is ready to take back its own

outside,
seagulls, raucous, complaining
inside
blurred signs
secrets

Catherine Edmunds
The Driftwood Tree, Circaidy Gregory Press

The Leopard-God

Came the Leopard-God
in a cape of beech leaves:
from one shore to the other
he passed at night,
with Nicholas on his back
clutching the fur and crying,
come again, come back,
pulling at the linty ears
of the Leopard-God – who
never gets angry, or at least
not with Nicholas, his own
blond boy, his refugee – his
little, his ever-so-patient love.

Chloe Stopa-Hunt
White Hills, Clinic Publishing

From Professor Murasaki's Notebooks on the Effects of Lightning on the Human Body

89. Incident on the Horikiko Coast (30/07/78)

Young couple alone, he recumbent on red rock
near pinnacle of sand-hill pocketed with grass,
she by his feet, sky making threat of raindrops
though earth remaindered dry. Mid-afternoon,
adjacent to sun's zenith, she touching ground
at plural potions of her body, while lightning
conflaged cracked dead-bush 6m from stone,
surge entering body by left toe and knee-skins
scorched but hardly. Consciousness abandoned
but resumed itself to her beyond thirty minutes
bequeathing no damage but burn marks, livid
at spine terminus, shaping like shouting throat.
Her memories of suction into light fibrillating
like new leaves. Man felt no perverse effects,
seven heart-flowers uncorrupted in his hand,
though since he suffers rapture of tympanum.

213. Higashi-Yuri-Machi Incident (22/09/97)

In Takaiwa-Yama, summer's declining parts,
school-teacher of language and nine-year son
relaxing in garden by lotus pool at light-fade,
playing go. No hailstones, no St. Elmo's Fire,
so foreboding invalid, yet flash strick jay-tree
20m distance, beneath whose roots iron pipe
reclined, convoying pool-water at arid times.
Predominant currents swept below go-board
and players either side, with subsidiary flow

up left leg of father, departing from his body
at index, central fingers of right hand almost
touching board. They badly cindered, fused,
yet still holding black stone for further play.
There is death in the ha-ne, as proverb says.
Boy hurtled into water, naked as carried out,
unscathed except for fern-prints on left heel.

John Latham
From Professor Murasaki's Notebooks on the Effects of Lightning on the Human Body, Comma Press

Camp 4

No sign of life
not a bird, not a plant.
Only lichens clothing
the sharp stones with grey.

A patch as big as a penny
can be more than a century old
here in this place
where vegetation is at rest
350 days of the year.

Deriving nourishment
chiefly from stone

the lichen is thus a plant
which in all its poverty
has eternity before it.

Autumn Richardson
Heart of Winter, Corbel Stone Press

Artillery

Artillery Memorial, Hyde Park Corner

Unexplode the shell.
Let its shrapnel rehome,
let it fly the six thousand yards
– line, no man's land, line –
back into the hot muzzle
of the eighteen pounder.

Let the gunner
heft it out, cold,
swing, let go, rebuild the pile.
Reload the limbers,
assemble the gun team,
summon the gypsy horses,
back to the base at Saigneville,
Dannes or Outreau.

To the tubs.
Let the cranes weigh down
the ship, the ship
sail coast to coast,
unburden itself
onto train, truck.

To the Filling Factory
at Woolwich, Chilwell or Banbury.

Listen. Listen
to the Canary sing
while she unfills the shell,
her face bright

as the hair
that escapes her scarf,

or the flash
that accompanies
a sudden release
of energy
on the surface
of an adolescent star.

Vanessa Gebbie
Memorandum: Poems for the Fallen, Cultured Llama

Simplifying My Mother

I'm attempting to simplify my mother

Going through her cupboards
Unwrapping bag within bag
In her dust-laden bedroom

Finding the odd photo
A faded guarantee
A broken hanger
A scrap of paper
With an address or name

A glove or lotion preserved
For some special occasion

Which never came

I could draw my mother's decline
On a map of her local area -
Circles or contour lines
Of smaller and smaller radius

Ray Diamond
A Barrel of Monkeys, Dempsey & Windle

Eva, Homo sapiens ssp. Brokenheart

A notice on her compound reads – 'May bite – please do not feed' –
although she drew her teeth in protest at the trade in ivory.
She carved a tusker's name on each and wears them round her neck.

She's tucked behind the tapirs and sloths, but from the viewing deck
you'll see her fingers swarm to tend the ghosts of bears, lost
when the polar ice caps warmed. All she sees are shadows since her eyes
drowned in the floods. They've stuck electrodes to her chest, its rise
and fall as rapid as the squeak of pipistrelles. Her heart stopped
when the last Sumatran Tiger died. The shock waves felled trees

across the zoo. At half past five, when all the viewers leave,
she sings in voices of the past – po'ouli's secret chit chit chit, the
quagga's plaintive bray, the thylacine's whine and yip yip yip.

They're kind to her. She has a chair, a bed, a diet of soaps and crime.
They've matched her with a mate, a specimen from Seoul. He's in his prime.

Jan Harris
Journeys Beyond, Earlyworks Press

Soho Hens

They teeter in deeleyboppers, sashed,
from one fun to another, trashed
on Flaming Sambucas in the afternoon.
They jostle like a silvery balloon
bouquet tethered to a jittery child.
Fit to explode, juiced and wild,
they karaoke meaning every word
till, sad as daylit tinsel, with homeward-
leaning hearts, in glad migration
they wheelycase it to the station,
wanting their mums, longing to be
in slippers, made a proper cup of tea.

Kathy Pimlott
Goose Fair Night, The Emma Press

from Still

A confined space is constructed, its entrance restricted,
Its roof sealed, a slatted window opened to each wall
Facing the four winds, allowing angled light.
A bullock with two-years' growth to his horns is singled out:
He thrashes and bucks as they plug his nostrils and mouth
Then pound him with blunt blows
Till his flesh and organs are mush but the hide stays whole.
With a bed of branches under his ribs
And wild thyme and cassia pods scattered about
They shutter him in and leave him to rot.
This works best when the first west wind of the year
Musses the lake, before the meadow blushes
And the swallow moulds its igloo under the eaves.
As the season builds, a sticky essence swelters and brews
In the sweet marrow of the beast's bones,
Till suddenly an astonishment of bees burst forth,
Flightless, then agitating their wings into life,
Thirsting for dew, testing the ways of the air
Until they swarm and climb, veiling the sky
Like a summer downpour, or go bulleting past.

Simon Armitage
Still, Enitharmon Press

Beirut
To Mona Saudi

My childhood taught me the alphabet.

Beirut taught me the language of life,
for her I raise an altar in my heart.

How does a city come to be in pain,
like you and I?

Beirut city of the soul, my body embraces you.
What am I –

observer or witness?
Can I stop consciousness knocking on my heart?

What can we do to stem the flood?

In Beirut I saw the walls of the world
built with bombs, with burning iron.

In Beirut I understood the meaning of life.
I touched the human essence.

Beirut, O remain with me
protect the rhythm of my soul.

For the sake of hope,
of a just world without walls.

Fathieh Saudi
Daughter of the Thames, Exiled Writers Ink

Green Girls

Wriggling on the bottles:
Drink us, drink us,
green girls

tell you water
is the long hair that you
swallow.

Whistle all you want,
a girl who swims this water
will make you swallow.

But if you tell her no,
(Not no, not no,)
then water's all you've got.

Lonely on a rock
the green girls do their writhe,
Drink me, drink me –

it's dark inside,
inside the inside,
deep inside the green girls.

There's a thirst inside
the green girls
you can't wait to find, no,

running down your windshield
coming from behind.
They're nymphs

you'd like to drink,
Drink us, drink us.
Oh the green girls want to die.

Down the drain, down –
help us, help us down the drain.
No one knows what's inside.

It's dark inside,
inside the inside,
deep inside the green girls,

there's a thirst inside
the green girls you really
want to ride.

Terese Svoboda
Professor Harriman's Steam Air-Ship, Eyewear Publishing

The Boat

i.m. Seamus Heaney

Take the case of a man in a boat
in deep water. The wind and the waves
and the craft's tossing cause him to stumble
if he makes to stand up, for, no matter how firmly
he tries to hold on, through the boat's slithering
he bends and he staggers, so unstable
the body is. And yet he is safe.

It's the same with the righteous:
if they fall, they are falling only
like a man in a boat who is safe and sound
as long as he stays within the boat's timbers.

Piers Plowman, passus 8

Bernard O'Donoghue
The Seasons of Cullen Church, Faber & Faber

Mal de Mer

The sea was heaving,
he threw up
a starfish
and a bivalve mollusc
(it was the clam before the storm).

He began
roiling and boiling
and thrashing and crashing
and bashing the rocks
and lashing the shore.
He awoke the kittiwakes
and scared all the buoys and gulls.

Sick of himself,
sick of making waves,
he went out
and took some deep breaths.

When he came back in
he was feeling fine,
quite well,
just swell.

Emma Purshouse
I Once Knew a Poem who Wore a Hat, Fair Acre Press

The Man Who Ran Through the Tunnel

When I heard
how he ran
across continents
over rivers
through forests
through deserts
and through tunnels,
how could I fail
to be inspired?

Ambrose Musiyiwa
Over Land, Over Sea: poems for those seeking refuge,
Five Leaves Publications

Dear Margaret

For Orgreave, the Beanfield, and Hillsborough.
For Operation Swamp '81.
For rejoicing in the burning and drowning of men.
For the miners, the unions,
the working class heroes,
the people whose skin you denied.
For the innocents turned into criminals.
For giving the Force a free rein
to wield batons and tear gas and horses,
to weaken and batter them all.

For the families who died.
For the lies you allowed to be told
all this time, never giving an ounce
of the truth or of justice for this 96.
For the mass destruction of all our communities,
psyches and spirits and faith.

For my dad, ex-Services, thrown on the dole
fifteen times in as many long months.

For my mother, dug deeper in poor mental health;
the poverty making her sicker, and sadder,
and madder than she'd ever been.

For my brother, who lived without wages for years,
burned out
on a pyre of your making.

For the youth of myself, for the public disgrace
of the free-dinner-queue,

for the old cast-off shoes,
for none of the school trips or cookery lessons.
For the shrinking grey socks, for the punches and kicks
that my mother let fly in her madness.

For the ice and the mould inside every window.
For the hunger, the shame, my family's pain,
for the living we scraped hand-to-mouth.

For all the above, for all our lost years,
for all of the grief and the depths that we reached,

Dear Margaret,

there's no absolution,
no forgiveness, or pity or grief.
Your legacy lives in the fat of the rich.
May your soul never find any peace.

Laura Taylor
Kaleidoscope, Flapjack Press

Above Antarctica

I've circled this research station a million times
in darkness, a million times in daylight
to send your messages home ...*So far away...I miss you...*

Not long left now... Save. Send. Wait for a response.
I relay your metadata on ocean warming
and thinning ice to labs across the world. *Nowhere*

too far away. Your observations of this continent
attuned to my wavelength. Spectrometer readings.
Fossil discoveries. Aurora activity. Solar flares.

Snowfall. Open a new spreadsheet. Save.
Fill in a hundred cells. Click send. Quick.
Not long left now. What can we save?

I orbit on towards the dark horizon.

Nancy Campbell
This is one of five special commissions, on the National Poetry Day 2016 theme 'messages', from poets shortlisted for the Felix Dennis Prize for Best First Collection,
Forward Arts Foundation

Coast

You and I in the rattling house
set far out at the edge of fields,
marking the end of the narrow road.

The touchstone of the latch,
opens onto the long dune grass
and empty yellow sand.

Two miles to walk to the nearest shop,
along a beach path, we find what the
sea has left, green rope, broken boxes,

perfect eye socket
in the bone head of a bird.
In the petrol chugging of a lobster boat,

the fall of a rock is a shout,
the shingle sifts, in the
tide.

The water brings to the door
what it found on other shores,
flotsam of washed out plastic,

bottles written in different languages,
that float like anemones,
abandoned in brown crab pools.

Wind burns the edge of morning.
No longer landlocked, come back
to the place we came from.

Flare from a flint, the sky endless. We
hear our breath in the salted light, an
ancient shanty of earth and air.

Clare Crossman
The Frogmore Papers 87, The Frogmore Press

When Guests Came

You'd give the gravelled instruction,
don't tell, then slip me a thimble of rum.
The crushed hat wore you tilted
like the lampshade with the brown blemish
made to face the wall when guests came. Rum
greased your heels, suds worked into mouth corners
with sweet talk of a horse named sugar water
& walking the corn-starched roads of back home.
You'd drop the limp you called a spring, turn
the volume down on your accent; the two-forty-five
at Epsom and give the man who pummelled
your daughters face into a slab of clay
your seat at the head of the dinner table.

Natacha Bryan
Lighthouse 12, Gatehouse Press

How I Was Born

In the bathhouse we women shed
panties and socks like skin,
our bodies, moons at full bloom.
The *onsen*: spring waters well
from granite throats. Pools wait,
murky with minerals.
We slip into them, bodies tattooed
with wrinkles, stretch marks ripple
on thighs like high tides.
Our arms slick as soap stone
are pale oars churning the waters.
My mother smiles at me.
Her breasts bowed from nursing,
shoulders curved, a ship's hull.
My grandmother, her pale hand
a compass directing me to shore.
They empty buckets on my back,
water coursing with secrets.
Some say we're formed in water
birthed like ships thrust out to sea.
But I was born
among these women,
a stone burnished –
passed from hand to hand.

Sayuri Ayers
Radish Legs, Duck Feet, Green Bottle Press

Foetiverse

... systematic enterprise builds & organizes knowledge through testable
explanations and predictions about the universe ...
(Science)

... let it be a beautiful confusion ...
(I. Flesh et al)

as both foetematic
buildanizing of knowenizable
systeprises & uniable organiversalisation
functionality entermatically explamatic in sub-
supra buildictions show   testidictable
organilds missysteprise & refoetivize uniatic
throughanations both with untestiversarily pre-pro-bi-
co-resystematic orgaprises
& subsize-a-testaprizeables whilst andiversering
trans-explaverse enteranation co-re-predictionationally
misthoughanizless
pre-re-testexpleledgentions at the superintersectings
of co-mid-testiverse entermatics without interexplamatory
semianderprisable systables explaniziful within
sub-supra-nonorganildic misfoetematicing cotestilanities
as dis-un-pre-de-refoetematicalisationalarilly
semi-intra-non-missysteprisemizenaliations both
sub-re-un-mis-interorganitestiversanizeiserates &
pre-de-dis-uni-mis-de-co-
enteranderpriseiversaniamaticisanizelessnessmentlying
semisubmisdisunderdefoetandtestan-
alisobuildiversaprisanaizeapriselizeingly
equi-mis-bis-syste-predi-re-di-co-build-ildi-
inimalisationary-ise-ationative-erilly
cross-free-orga-re-bi-iso-
mistisystebuildiversidiesanal-
aprisanizeaprisalizes
then the foetiverse

Serafina Palic
Science Foetus Foetus Science, GUG Press

Her Publisher

I love this time of year, time of day:
the light, pale-egg and misty; platform
almost empty. Malcolm says we'll wander,
find somewhere nice for lunch. We always do:
Italian spaghetti, a carafe
of red wine. I'll have to watch my frock.
I love all the bustle of Soho,
like another planet. The awards
don't start till 6. And, do you know, I don't
even mind meeting the Queen, the mood
I'm in. Plus, I put the milk bottles out
already, and extra food for Saturn.

Malcolm's eyes are the colour of clear sky.
I'm sure to make the 11:03.

Charlotte Gann
Noir, Happen*Stance* Press

This Feels Right

I'm surprised when I think how easily
I settled into the life experience as
a child – accepted everything. I mean
nothing unsettled me – the sky, the sun
and moon, seasons changing – even people
seemed natural enough. Washing, eating,
laughing, crying, our gorgeous tabby cat,
all seemed perfectly normal. It was almost
as if I'd been here before. Then I started
school and everything changed.

Paul Birtill
New and Selected Poems, Hearing Eye

from Canto II, Hammersmith

Once more you emerge in the autumn light
For find your parents' London gone
From the streets where the gasping buses grind on

To no fixed abode, where is no stay,
Not known at this address,
Or never known, or went away,

Gone where the post eventually goes,
With the midnight flit or the number
Forgotten for want of a pencil just then

On the dim top landing or under a streetlight
At closing. In this way their city is lost
With all the lives they might have led.

You want to go home. But you have to begin.
Here now at noon you must empty the Broadway
Of all but the dead, and set out

From the unquiet shade of the lime-tree
As if you must know where you're going,
As if you might even belong.

Sean O'Brien
Hammersmith, Hercules Editions

Boa Senior Has Died

In memory of a survivor of the tsunami
and the last speaker of Bo

When the wave came down upon them
Boa Senior climbed.
The elders told us the earth would part.
Don't move or run away.

The wave broke with a heavy sound.

From her tree she looked
as dogs and children
and stoves and walls and bicycles
flowed slowly past. Her roots clung.

Afterwards, she climbed down
and sat on the damp sand,
arms folded around her knees.
She saw branchless trees and a still sea.

She didn't say anything.

Six years later, her dry language
would die when she died.
Now it lay on her tongue.
She bit her lip and pushed the words
against the inside of her teeth.

Arabella Currie
IRIS: A Collaboration, Hurst Street Press

Portrait of the Lover #4

Stephen Emmerson
Family Portraits, if p then q

Dead Poet at the Swimming Pool

Outside rain clatters through gutters
pays thick ropes through gratings, drains

and still he's here, hunched on the steps, his head
hanging in his hands. No one takes any notice

Not the receptionist in her office
pool staff swabbing dingy floors, slick-haired men

fraught mothers trailing dripping kids with neon wings
all too preoccupied

to clear his eyes of silt and withered leaves
his dirt-stopped mouth

It's early autumn when she kneels beside him
drops a coin to gauge the depth

ten more years before she hears it
hit the bottom

Deborah Harvey
Breadcrumbs, Indigo Dreams Publishing

Threads

I once said we were connected by a thread,
fine and strong and silken as a spider spins.
Though there have been times I've felt I had instead
a coarsely-cabled rope chafing round my limbs.

And there have been times I could have cut it clean,
cast myself blind, without reasons or goodbyes
from our world's rim, without you to reel me in,
and fallen seed-free to unknown galaxies.

I never did: heart was made marionette
as you spoke (like child into a paper cup,
string held taught) words barely registered, but yet
resonated. I backed up; my blade grew blunt.

I once said we are connected by a thread,
but I was wrong it is a web, patched and grown
as life's loom shuttles on, each fresh synapse
sequin sewn and charting a galaxy known.

Nathan Evans
Threads, Inkandescent

Vocabulary

winter closing in …
I visit the simplest words
in the dictionary

*

where my vocabulary clouds clouds

*

this cold morning's
ghost of a meaning
in steam from the tops
of tall buildings

*

deep within
the falling snow
a truer word for it

Philip Rowland
Something Other Than Other, Isobar Press

[extract]

12. Andrea's house had cherry-print
    curtains in the bedroom, on which
    Oll once wiped his mouth

13. Souad's house had a Victorian-
    style street lamp in the front garden

14. Helen's house is a bungalow with
    an upstairs, but that's Helen all
    over

15. Kemi's house is on a corner, and
    her other house is also on a corner

16. Jason's house was opposite a flat
    belonging to an uninhibited woman

17. Gillian's house has a kitchen
    extension

18. Leona's house is pleasant and
    ordinary, but that's Leona all over

19. Linda's house is full of elephants

Rachel Sills
Two Hundred Houses, Knives Forks and Spoons Press

from **du Bellay (3)**

Before I was voted Head of Department,
At the worst possible moment in the
University's fifty year history,
I used to follow the steep path of Shakespeare and Dante,
Lifted up by the wings of poetry.
Now there's a sign reading FOOTPATH CLOSED,
And I have a stuffed in-tray to keep me busy,
So must tread a different road,
And learn to hold my tongue at Leadership Away-Days.
That's why, Schmidt, having missed the road that Maxwell
Followed to St. Lucia and back,
I am earwitness to the ordinary noise,
Lacking the strength and the puff to follow, like him,
The flight path that leads to Walcott's villa.

Philip Terry
du Bellay, Chapbook Anthology: Volume One, Laudanum

from Broken it shows inside a kind of buttery filling

Broken it shows inside a kind of buttery filling, as if all along its roboticality was only on the outside, they were not after all mechanisms but soft things with flows and runs of sense. But perhaps I thought this only applies to the larger insects, in smaller ones the liquidity is no more than a smear, that can hardly, I thought, speak of animal passions. Each awn wants, to feel is to ride the sentence out where in the dust, limbs strut and tent. Only as verb does mind name something real, in the empire of the sensible on a typestract at x ideaspersecond. Daddy Longlegs belongs with that troupe of wrestlers from 70s Saturday afternoons, Giant Haystack etc. I considered how a windshield's starcrack is already bugred, gunshot-holed. A scrapmetal spectre, wrought by fingers of air, one of its regional names was 'pull-the-legs from me'. I slept a fragment, how the hungry mirrors have the voice of the ocean and contain each word in every language, but never utter a sound. The glove of me is lost in upflows to self, lost in a crowd the great life-poem that writes its knowledge, the flaps of me in trees caught the blind light of the stars when the clouds impersonate dreams and aerial drones divetail the eyes' extent.

Giles Goodland
Broken it shows inside a kind of buttery filling,
The Literary Pocket Book

Lunch on Omaha Beach

The killers are killed, their violent rinds
Conveyed, and the beach is back to summer.
I eat sausage with bread. Full of ease, the sea
Makes the sound of cows chewing through high grass.

They're deposited in government lawn
Set with nine thousand decencies of stone
To wet the eye, shake the heart, and lose
Each name in a catalog of graven names.

They are wasted in the blank of herohood.
They are dead to fondness and paradox.
They're all the same. In the field of lawn
Above the beach, they're put away the same.

They should be left exactly here below where
Death's great bronze mares shook earth and bloodied them,
Where violence of noise isolated each boy
In the body of his scream, and dropped him.

No worn Norman hill should be scarred and smoothed
To suit officials' tidy thoughts for graveyards
But the wreckage left, shrinking in rust and rags
And carrion to dust or tumuli.

To honor my thoughts against shrines, to find
The beast who naked wakes in us and walks
In flags, to watch the color of his day
I spill my last Bordeaux into the sand.

Watching, I wonder at the white quiet,
The fields of butter cows, my countrymen
Come to study battle maps, blue peasants
Still moving back and forth, the day's soft sea.

Bink Noll
The House and Other Poems, Little Island Press

Phlegmatic

She rattles her choked ribs
up from graffitied streets,
where sentences that roam market walls
and hoardings round stored land
read like the stale breath of banked air,

to where spray won't be penned,
paint finds no purchase,
and claims spelt out in mass footfall
proved heartier than purse or word.

Here at the wet-lashed gape
of this caged lung she hears it:
bluster and fall, trickled whisper
to broad-throated roar;
feels its spit brush her,
stroke her clear.

Fay Musselwhite
Contraflow, Longbarrow Press

Calais

This mud is different.
Were I writing home
I'd struggle to describe
its darker pigment,
how it slips beneath our feet,
a long, slow slide
where boots lose grip.

Under our sheeting
we listen to the rain;
traffic on the near road
lets out a groan, a hiss.
We have learned the art
of slow patience,
of being still, endlessly.

There is always tomorrow,
always the chance
that there will be movement.
Today we cheered
when someone's phone
showed a man walking
out of a tunnel's darkness.

Nicholas Murray
The Migrant Ship, The Melos Press

Just a Nobody

The dead man was no one,
just a man in tattered clothes,
no shoes,
just a coin in his pocket,
no id cards, no bus ticket.
He was a nobody,
dirty and skinny,
a no one, a nobody
who clenched his hand before he died.
When they pried open his fingers,
this nobody,
they found a whole country.

Hama Tuma (trans. from Amharic by the author)
MPT The Great Flight, Modern Poetry in Translation

Graves' Disease
after 'Down Among The Empty Boats', Sonia Lawson

Her clothes are the texture
of congealing blood.
She would like to do it,
to gouge out
the hungry shuddering thing
in her throat, let her life
seep away beside the quay,
where the hollows of empty boats

echo inside her.

But her abdomen is distended
by motherhood.
She must latch on to this
matter – the glimpse of red
in the boat nearest her, a child's
tipped-up bucket, sand teeming
out like time; a spade –
she must make them matter.

Becky Cherriman
Echolocation, Mother's Milk Books

Walking the Ridgeline

To be here at last, catching your breath
    from crossing the ridge,
poised between one valley and another,

watching the sun fall under the horizon's blanket,
    while the wind sheers and veers to North
            carving age into your face like a blade on ice.

    Landmarks are indistinct --
symbols on the map of the journey here,
        the way you catch the flash in the darkening

down there in the distance,
        the sign of something coming,
                        or going,

        as headlights turn a corner,
and you hear the mistle thrush singing premonitions
                        of night.

Is this ridgeline
            just words and the sky pouring off
                        the edge of the horizon?

The smudge of smoke from dying hillside heather fires?
            The faint hum of car wheels
                        on a failing road?

    Or the shadows of leafless trees,
at that border between field and forest,
                        creeping closer?

Perhaps it's time to come down off the hill,
close the curtains on this dark, keep the heat in,
lay the fire, hope for warmth --

give up counting days,
or breaths,
one by one.

Robin Moss
Walking the Ridge Line, Mudfog Press

Basic Training

It was Zero Week when they rattled
our heads up and down like Etch A Sketches,

erasing lines and dissolving connections,
but only later did I realize how

significantly we all changed.
At the time I thought I knew

what was happening because
men always believe they're in control.

The changes were subtle, like how
you're enjoying a beautiful sunset

when suddenly you look around
and it's dark outside.

Lucas Shepherd
Neon Literary Magazine issue 43, Neon Books

Three Haiku

ACCORDION HAIKU

Sound of an accordion
Flying above the railway
Shadow of a crow

Vanessa Vie
Lyrical Soulmates, New Departures/Poetry Olympics

UK IN-OR-OUT REFERENDUM HAIKU

Ligging snug in own
Bed – or non-swimmer in deep
End's a No-brainer

Michael Horovitz
Lyrical Soulmates, New Departures/Poetry Olympics

THE SENTINEL

On the look-out post
Atop the fishmonger's van
A single seagull

Vanessa Vie & Michael Horovitz
Lyrical Soulmates, New Departures/Poetry Olympics

Painting
She ain't holding them up, she's holding on
(some English Rose) by Sonia Boyce 1986

I saw my mother in this painting of Sonia Boyce;
the woman wearing a red dress with black roses,
holding her family above her head – a basket of life.
And like her she was holding us up,
her load no lighter for having two babies
out of wedlock, holding on, making a life
in strange places fighting the struggle of womanhood.

Love evaded her twice, men she couldn't hold on to,
no matter how wide she opened her heart.
Holding on to any job whilst handing over her babies
to be held by others until she returned, tired and weary.
Holding on to hope that a childless couple would take
care of the one she'd leave behind; knowing
that her last breath upon his skin would be a new beginning.

Roy McFarlane
Beginning With Your Last Breath, Nine Arches Press

Endless Trains

As we skirt Dartmoor, clouds nuzzle the landscape, and grey and green subtleties remind me I am keen to see the Agnes Martin exhibition, although Susan warned me that you have to relax into the work, otherwise it's easy to miss the faint colour and detail.

Some kind of conglomerate of drinkers join the train at different stations, seem to find each other by intuition before sharing bottles of prosecco and Hungarian plum and honey spirit, company notes across the aisle. Complex tattoos, piercings and pain, skin art on graffiti girls, all 80s ripped jeans and undersize leather jackets, attitude and chit chat.

They josh and boast the hours away with snacks and delicacies, more wine, and loud discussion about their futures. How do they know each other? Where are they going? They keep us entertained as we come up for air from sandwiches and books.

Why do I keep this notebook and not my drafts on paper? Why the expensive grids of vertical pages, this particular brand? Some sense of revealing process as well as final edits, some residual nostalgia for documenting trips: New York, London, Italy, endless trains to home.

Rupert M Loydell
Love Songs For An Echo, Original Plus

Number

It's the same for me today
as when we were eight or nine,
when Ronnie Smith created a distraction
from Mr Wandless's addition and subtraction
by bellowing
It's snowing!

Attention leapt to the window:
we gawped and sighed as pale flakes
dallied, floated down,
while those that drifted near the misted pane
rallied in the thermal lift.
Feathers from an eiderdown
multiplied and blanketed the cold playground.

Not mere dots, but clusters,
maybe half an inch across. They wafted
by the classroom, spangled grey sky;
their lightness glowed,
dividing wintry dreams from arithmetic,
more mystical than magic.

More than a hundred; more than a million;
more than the sum of all the pale white numbers
Mr Wandless ever chalked across a blackboard.
They added four inches to their depth by playtime.

And afterwards, we all — except Mr Wandless —
thawed out blue fingers that tingled
number than pins and needles, stuck deep into armpits.
We grinned at our shivering.

I feel that same grin as I ache by my window today,
quiver at the echo of a distant voice, rejoicing.
It's snowing.

Peter R White
Ways to Wander, Otley Word Feast Press

Colours

My great aunt, Lily, was born the year
the Whitechapel murder victims died.
She filled her garden with flowers –
fuschias, geraniums, african marigolds –
anything for some colour. One year
she painted the iron railings,
the wicker chairs, the window frames
and the garden bench pale pink.
Another year the paint was all blood red.
Every night, in her dreams, her second boy,
John the rear gunner, who died in a dogfight
over Tripoli, fell down the sky in flames.
All the sisters wore white at her wedding.
Lily told me the wrong things are what lasts.

Sue Boyle
Safe Passage, Oversteps Books

Correspondence as Writing System

Correspondence is a garland of skulls that may be divided absolutely into 1 or 2 or 3 or 4 or 10 or 50 or 51 or 108 or 1000 or 1008 skulls. This calculation is correct, repeatedly, to the point of vivisection.

For example, a mother as not less than measure as not less than authority as not less than light as not less than knowledge as not less than binding, fettering as not less than death as not less than a woman's waist.

This example is untimely, and stubbornly so; lazy returns painted on handicraft paper. Following pseudo-Vedic manuscripts, we apologise ourselves into disarticulation.

Survival disables the open mind.

We circulate stars: a dark blue transit, a counterfeit ring, a rosebush grows beneath the table.

Obstructed by the space that is saving for you, my interior distends: the first to the first, the blood to the blood, the divesting of colourless fields.

She is afflicted by this geological era insofar as her activities are the colour of spoiled meat. But the generally felt precedes the disgrace of seasoning.

Home is a collection of contagious
objects. She licks the lid of the project.

Nisha Ramayya

Correspondences, Oystercatcher Press

Sex Talk Among Women

On the way back from the Hamptons
we argue about language and sex,

how speech reduces women to the status
of a wall plate waiting for a plug.

Nail, screw, drive, thrust, penetrate, and *pork*.
We build our lives with words

and yet have never heard or read *engulf,*
surround, enfold.

We who last night bared
our bodies in the whirlpool are now divided

by the description of a penis.
You put the cover on the mayonnaise jar;

you don't put the jar in the cover.
    Yeah, but you put the jar in the refrigerator.

A refrigerator is a big, dumb, cold thing.
    Don't be angry -- that's so Seventies.

A circle of women, we sat in steam
celebrating beauty and differences,

the sizes of our breasts, the flatness
or curve of bellies, the shades

of our pubic hair.
Voices rise and sharpen.

We miss our exit bickering,
ask directions at a deli

selling *Let Christ Help You Beat Temptation*
bumper stickers, day-glo condoms, cans of worms.

Alison Stone
The Chronicles of Eve, Paper Swans Press

[untitled]

nature pursues you
from behind
in fantasies it mows the backyard
and spreads grass over the floor
with each swing of the scythe
bills are strewn
aromatically

beauty buys
reality

in poetic fantasies it mounts you
splits the body
and cashes in lilies

after the winter fee
the smell of spring

a sweaty copy of you
sighs

Elías Knörr aka Elias Portela
Greitt í liljum (Paid in lilies), Partus Press

#56.

I think you will let me run; you will follow walking
at a brisk pace; soon I will be out of breath,
soon the pain in my ankle and knees will slow me,
soon there will be a fence between me and escape,
soon I will wonder about my heart, and you
who know my name, you who can see my body's distress
will chuckle softly, watching me sit, watching me saying,
Okay, okay, okay, you got me – and maybe we will
laugh, and you will say, Man you need to lose some.

And I will roll on my stomach and welcome the soft
damp cool of the grass, and you will then put on
the cuffs, and I will say, Not so tight, and you will say
How's that? and I will say, Thanks, and Sorry, man,
just got freaked by the taser, and you will say,
You know that was some stupid shit you pulled,
and I will say, Yeah man, sorry, and you will say
I could have shot you, and something about being
pissed off and all the damned paperwork,
and even though I'd want to, I won't say,
All this over a broken tail light? or,
You know you wrong to stop me, but I will say
I used to run better, and you will say, Football?
And I will say, Yeah, we get fat after a while,
and then the sirens of the back-up will fill the air,
and my heart will sink, but will still be beating
and that will be the end of the day, see?

How optimistic and forgiving of me to cast this all
in the future tense, as if I have some dream that someday
this is how a Blackman and a white cop will laugh

on a sunny Charleston afternoon; how forgiving
of me to avoid the judgement of the subjunctive,
of the abstracted hope of what might have been,
when we know that what has been
is an indictment of what might have been.
Old sinner man, where yuh gonna run to?
Downpressorman, where yuh gonna run to,
on that day, on that day, on that day?

So you know, I ran from you. I will run from you,
I would run from you because I grow stupid
when I am around you, and you might ask me
who you is and all I can say is you is not me,
which is never enough, but we are talking about
what has been or what is to come or what should have,
which is another way of saying we can't do a thing
about any of it, except to know you is not me.

Kwame Dawes
Speak From Here To There, Peepal Tree Press

Cain Reverses Time

Cain's beard grows into Euclidean space:
its anchors catch on every form and drag them back.
He is a camera capacious enough to film the entire world
forever, and then rewound to unmake every wound.
I wait for it to stop once I am reunited with my family.
I fall asleep with my hand on her waist, our sons
on either side. I feel like an illustration on a jug.
But no. A suicide bomber is making a pasta collage.
He cries when his mum is the last one to pick him up.
A friend reverses all the way from the accident
to his last conversation about Tallis's *Lamentations*.
Nations slip inside nations like matryoshka dolls.
Oh, I see. I see what this is about. The fecund plains,
the scattered grain and oranges, almonds, passion fruit,
apples, berries, marrows, tomatoes, lychees
whip up and, in a reverse whirlwind, assemble neatly
on the grassy dais. But something is wrong.
Cain is not trying to reverse his decision, but God's.
An altar where a muscular lamb bleats ignored.
A shaft of light gutters, hesitates then settles in
to bathe Cain's offering in holy light. He
stands over his brother's body, a jawbone
in his fist, and we follow the drip of blood in, frankly,
melodramatic slow-motion. Thanks anyway.

Luke Kennard
Cain, Penned in the Margins

A Hum

A colony has been moved from the loft
this morning, the rafters scraped clear
of their stash of sticky gold.

Brick-sized ingots drip into buckets,
bowls overflow. The girl who cleans knows
honey's royal role in winter remedies

and how it keeps you young. Her grandma's
skin is soft as a baby's at eighty, she says.
Today, she's straining and storing the harvest

for the bankers who bought the house
with the honey in it. They know nothing about it,
she says. Just sniff at the mess.

They know even less about her, the help,
and the man who's followed her from Waterford,
erected a tent in their orchard.

How she trickles downstairs, slides into night,
belly brimming amber, trembling
to be touched, to be tasted.

How the tent walls billow,
how the orchard is flooded with light,
and the lovers are humming somewhere

outside of themselves, without names,
or addresses, on sweet rooty earth, where air
smells of honey musk, the heather in bloom.

By the end of the week, jars are sealed,
shelves stacked, tables scrubbed -
the kitchen reeks of Vim.

She is replete, still perfumed by him.
The bankers pay her to leave.

Cora Greenhill
Far From Kind, Pindrop Press

Memories of Ice

A strange amount of memorization is nothing like this song.

The amnesiac feels the exhilaration of waking, moment after moment.

I have worn out a memory of one night. I have broken

a word, I have broken.

The most preserved memory is that which is entombed, not relived.

Eroded and reshaped and reshaped I remembered, no

recalled, The morning is the mourning is the mourn and This

morn is nocturnal.

Joanna Doxey
Plainspeak, WY, Platypus Press

Interval

There's snow in the wind
and a plug of ice on the barrel.
I've come to love these local intensities,
the postman's step on the gravel,
four cats to feed, two chickens to water,
the washing-machine to empty,
the smell of clothes on the line,
wind-freshened!
The computer humming at ease.
I suppose it's on days like these
poems happen— between the chores,
the lists, and the breeze.

W.S. Milne
Poem Flyer 3, Poem Flyer

After the Storm

sunshine on late roses,
a queue of swallows on the wire,
the sky washed clean and spread to dry:
she finds his gloves in the hall-table drawer:
leather moulded to the curl of his palms.

The smell of him,
Left, right, she draws them on.
Key deep in one pocket, jar in the other,
she gathers boots, lead, walking stick.
The spaniel dances at the door.

On the hill the wind shakes leaves
and jackdaws out of the sycamores.
Her coat flaps flightless wings.
She climbs until the sea
rises into sight, a flake of silver.

The dog bounces through heather.
Clouds hurry into the east.
Her gloved hands unscrew the lid
and tilt the jar. The last of his dust
streams out on the wind.

Ama Bolton
Taking Notes: poems from Poetry Space Competition 2015,
Poetry Space

He Tells Tales of Meroe

As if his croak sounds from stone itself
As if his voice in darkness is stained with the timbre of eternity

When I first saw him alone, lost in thought,
poised behind glass,
I recalled how his sperm had oncespawned from the suck of motherly mud
to snatch prey with spit
A camouflaged trickster,
awakening each spring with his mates
to a spring of mating

Now an enigmatic relic behind glass,
perhaps he tells tales of Meroe –
witness to that city's sad trajectory from glory to dejection

In this, his last siesta,
he readies himself for life
with his new cloak, a new tongue and his crown

Al-Saddiq Al-Raddi
He Tells Tales of Meroe: Poems for the Petrie Museum,
Poetry Translation Centre

Her

When I said I like you this way:

- acrobat
- architect
- motion

I meant autoerotic, sunday afternoon,
heat. I meant orbital, clenched fists,
our concrete apartment /
accidents & bruised tongue

When I said I like you this way
I meant milk lapped,
you begging for what I couldn't,
vulpine & submissive in the only way.
I meant commitment
I meant strawberry red, accented,

vital

What are we waiting for?

Sophie Essex
Objects of Desire, PYRAMID Editions

A Boat of Letters

arrives, and I lie down in its white wet,
ink prints on my cheek, feet, and dress.
Last night I dreamt my husband
held me like a forceful wind
as I strained forward to hear
a group of girls sing soft, unclear,
in our doorway.
I pushed towards them. They seemed far away.
He was strong, and I struggled against him.
Boat of letters, filled to the brim,
take us to your wild inky swamp
where leaves hang down like muted lamps,
where we can write and read; and with each broken seal,
let there be an answer, a surprise, something delightful!

Eve Grubin
The House of Our First Loving, Rack Press

from Birdland

An image of the Engineer's model
shudders in a basement
as sand stabilisers are loaded.
The left arm bright gold, the ears glow green.
Out of its head energy spatialises
overlappings of spirallic fields.
A figure appears to attempt flight,
it may have wings, yet held to the floor
accelerates towards an openness through liberation
of its partner, unseen from the pit entrance.
Is it male? What is there to say
concerning child birth?
Its presence takes place
between table and pasture, at this moment
takes space between road and underground river:
it is named jouissance :
The arrival.
It brings experience of radical separation of self,
like child birth, produces an object of love.

Allen Fisher
Gravity as a consequence of shape, Reality Street

The Blank Page

Coming across a blank page
in a book of writing
like a sudden mist a clean bed sheet
or a loch reflecting November

I wondered was it deliberate tactics
on the part of the writer
like the point in a conversation
when one of us conceals our thinking

and we turn the page of the dialogue
and overleaf there are hundreds of words
to get lost in again almost forgetting
the threat and promise of that moment

and whether the absence was error or style.

Jim McGonigal
The Camphill Wren, Red Squirrel Press

The Light in the Winter Forest

The light in the winter forest
is low as an animal
it breaks around the trees like a prism:
white, pearly, almost smoke.
The long firs seem to stand in it
and all of it
has the 3am feeling of a nightclub
when too much has been taken or drunk or both
and everyone stops, their backs toward you
facing the booth, the strobe scanning them
waiting for the fall
and the tribal-tribal, terrible surrender
of a body dancing to earth, movement
so slow it looks like ticking. In Bavaria,
a friend calls it Brecht: the fractal fan of light
that strikes the wood into the water.
I think of the sparse prosody and the leaping runway,
the leaping, disappearing runway
and all the hours ahead.

Anna Selby
The Rialto 86, The Rialto

Fondant Cake

This fondant cake is here for you. A crisp, almost brittle crust, and a rich and dark crumb. Also this grief bacon.

Lila Matsumoto
Allegories from my Kitchen, Sad Press

Poem in Which I Am Not Shortsighted

First: surely myopia is a priestly calling,
where the world falls short in long isinglass halls.
Here souls flit like floaters, intransigent,
and the clear image crystallises forward
of the retina, oracular as a twist in a marble.

Secondly: resolution will never come to pass.
Even the finest lasers freeze at this degree
of negativity. It's easier to see myself eyeless,
orbits cored and caved. But I am tempted:
I imagine such a poem, and I want in.

Thirdly: short sighting's a matter of too much,
the whole 3-D backstory, the eye so stretched
it's water-sculpted as a barrel jellyfish.
At 20:20 it would all be different: my eyes
round as real globes, doll-painted, factory-fresh.

I admit that I once woke on a coach without lenses,
and at four a.m. could read the green LED
of the driver's clock. It was a temporary cure,
but it was fine: the ripping away of cloth;
miracle, with its tinsellish, lottery-win tocsin.

Judy Brown
Crowd Sensations, Seren

Norfolk Hawker

"The Norfolk Hawker is a delight to study. This is because places that are good for Norfolk Hawkers are also good for other species of dragonflies, notably Hairy dragonfly, Scarce Chaser and Variable Damselfly"
– Field Guide to the Dragonflies and Damselflies of Great Britain and Ireland.

Hello, hello, look at the size of that Devil's Darning Needle
 which, like a lack of sleep, will tack and tack
from your double take. Such darters, hoverers, skimmers, chasers,
 fly like a flag that flaps in four directions.

You know 350 million years ago they survived
 our beginnings as moron amphibians;
we were scarcely out of the water when
 these poster-tubes were whizzing around.

Spindly little chaps their larvae are, though
 they have a chip on their shoulder;
they will try to eat anything and that can be their undoing.
 We must stay low and still and slow and they see you

long before you see them – just there
 she's landed in the water soldiers' longer leaves.
Fully grown there's a ginger glint
 to their wishing-well-penny skins.

You can become quite obsessed quite quickly.
 The upturned exuvia is a perfect perspex replica.
Imagine one of these decoys, it'd be prisoner's delight.
 See you over the pond, by the wind-secluded water's edge,

or free at last; to bank and twist and hunt in Brampton Wood,
            Pip-pip like Pinewood's pilots, *Good Luck*,
leave the uncanny cases to go for a Burton
            on August's storms' damn, blast and double blast.
For any of you Norfolk Hawkers still alone along the broads
            your exhibition cases are the stuff of natural history.

Harry Man
Finders Keepers, Sidekick Books

Perfect Miming

Bad start: the microphone's broken.
He's so softly spoken
That people have thought he was miming
This is dreadful timing.

There's a good crowd – about 20,
Which experience tells him is plenty
But the chances of hearing him
Are very, very, very slim.

At the end, everyone claps
And he wonders if perhaps
He should abandon the spoken word
And perfect his talent for being unheard.

Neil Laurenson
Exclamation Marx!, Sihouette Press

Campanile
for Ben Reynolds

Sicked-over folk trembling, casts its fly too thick.
Wrung out of matter delight is limply purple and scoots
its dear trend song of hut culture, tubular.

What drops for the scaffold erected on skin islet
blooded by rain and the swelling pond,
the bracketed launch of the self-same

Or the sleaze of hut-ethics recognition, the bulbous
wood lodging's easy pickings? Are you complicit
as the brim of that desire, its muscular surety
its determined goers

Onwards
carouses the flannel to chlorine health kick,
the colour demanding gratitude is slick in bell-sheen
wolfed down as how it is-like prosody makes
shimmers attend/undulate.

The light's glance
knowing this pleasure to waver
that life either's stopped or is
stopped, is for you.

Tom Betteridge
Pedicure, SINE WAVE PEAK

Swimming with Jellyfish

For fun, the dolphins race the prow,
flip their white bellies over
for the crowd, some of whom run

from one side to the other. Even
his wife smiles, gripping the rail.
After, she drives them up the coast.

The balcony of their flat seems suspended
in the sea fret. She goes to lie down.
On the beach, sun presses to get through.

Families have parasols. Kids are netting
jellyfish: in a dinghy full of water,
they are pulsing like hearts, red

on yellow plastic. Wanting to be stung,
he swims into coolness. His fingers flinch
as he brushes them but he pushes on.

He thinks gentle breaststroke might save him –
a jellyfish drifts through his arms, kisses
his cheek. He splashes as if his feet

are tangled but no one can see him.
The ocean grows darker feeding on
the pale mist. Trawling a wake behind,

he makes the beach. The kids have vanished.
Jellyfish on sand, their buoyancy and gloss,
a gritty blob. Too late for them.

In the mirror, his face stares back.
On the raised skin, a red line,
an incision, tingling like an electric shock.

His wife gets antiseptic, cleans and cleans it,
doesn't ask why, rests her fingertips
on the exact place he'd been stung.

Stuart Pickford
Swimming with Jellyfish, smith|doorstop Books

For This Freedom

For this freedom of song beneath the rain
we'll need to give it all
For this freedom of being closely tied
to the sweet, steady insides of the people
we'll need to give it all
For this freedom of sunflower open in the dawn of factories
switched on and
  schools lit
and of earth creaking and child awakening
we'll need to give it all
There is no alternative but freedom
There is no other way but freedom
There is no other homeland but freedom
There will be no more poem if not for the violent music of
  freedom
For this freedom which is the fear
of those who always violated it
in the name of magnificent miseries
For this freedom which is the night of the oppressors
and the definitive dawn of all the people now invincible
For this freedom revealing the sunken pupils
 the bare feet
 the leaky roofs
 and the eyes of children who
wandered in the dust
For this freedom which is the empire of youth
For this freedom
beautiful like life
we'll need to give it all
if necessary

even shadow
and it will never be enough

Fayad Jamís
Nothing Out of This World: Cuban Poetry 1952-2000,
Smokestack Books

Broken English

Sometimes the English is broken
and I don't fix it.
Like the bone that snapped
after a misplaced step sent her tumbling.
It left the elbow at an angle
it was not designed to hold.
The joint that healed
(while she lay in the camp for the displaced)
grew too much cartilage,
and is stronger now
in that broken place.

Sometimes the English is broken
and I leave it.
Like the cracked glass with shards
refracting more rainbow
than the pane could ever hold.

Sometimes the English is broken
and I sit with it.
Listen to its song.
She has taken the time to
hold another's tongue
in her mouth. Felt it sit
like a slug at the back of her teeth,
but did not vomit.
Held it in place. Held her breath,
exhaled, and let the words out
for the others who could not come.

Sometimes the English is broken
and I look,
pin the impulse to fix frayed edges.
The visible stitches are his;
disappearing words hastily sewn
before they evaporate.
This skill, the last echo
of a previous life as a tailor, mending men.

Sometimes the English is broken
and I watch it

Juliana Mensah,
Dream Catcher 33, Stairwell Books

Blackwater

A little after dawn, the estuary
still as a tin dish of milk

and the air astringent, like a pain so true
it must just be borne.

On the mudbank, brent geese
talk gentleness to one another

their soft round voices
like small observed thoughts afloat

over the gunmetal
of the flats, the sheepwool snags of mist.

To look out over water
is the sweetest beginning

even in memory
even when you lie between walls.

Paul Blake
A Massacre of Hummingbirds, Stonewood Press

Unkanye (a poem for Christmas)

The true meaning of Christmas is Kanye West
Who has left his materiality behind and entered the realm of ideas
To live in a way that is beyond my comprehension
Every single positive thought in the universe is Kanye
As is every positive feeling and good deed. Every sweet nothing whispered
From lover to lover is Kanye the master of the internet; who invented the internet
Who administers the internet; who substitutes his brain for the internet
When the internet is recharging. Kanye kisses himself & the purest love ever known
Sweeps across the earth. What force can withstand the energy unleashed by Kanye
Kissing Kanye??? No force. The energy is the energy that moves us all that causes us all
To be the best that we can be and to achieve our daily greatness. Kanye kissing Kanye
Would be the best kiss on earth as it would be in heaven, ever, for always and for all time
Thereafter. Amen

Richard Barrett
LOVE LIFE!, Stranger Press

The Parting Glass

in memory of Adam Lewis

Now you've really torn the arse out of it
And all my best words can't make you less dead,
Our big reunion, our chance to kick-start
New times becomes a last visit instead –
No trains to book, no hint your heart could quit
Though all the while, unknown, the sickness spread –
No more missed calls or casual laughter,
Not even a joke – forever after.

I skipped your funeral. Sorry, but then
You hated protocol. I could not grieve
As others do, but came across you again
In a backstreet pub, your ghost at my sleeve
And there, oh how we talked, what time we passed,
As if each glass, my friend, could be our last.

Neil Young
The Parting Glass, Tapsalteerie

The Swell

Drum-tight, she looked about to burst.

He made a fuss of her for a change,

waded in wearing galoshes

as her waters broke, flooding

the house, leaving us to stay with strangers.

Up to our necks in silt. He tapped his hard hat,

made milk-dribble jokes for cameras,

said storms with girls' names were the deadliest.

Then she emerged, fresh with her slake

of new flesh as the whole town lugged sandbags,

trying to stop her.

Jessica Mookherjee
The Swell, Telltale Press

You Celebrate the Magnificence of Brunelleschi's Dome

yet struggle with the vaulted belly of a pregnant woman
and rummage inside your tote bag for an alter cloth
or a fire blanket to smother its fecundity.
You say I don't understand showing it off that way,
doused black or white to blur the curves is fine
but the trend these days for crop tops,
leaves no interface between belly and eye.
I don't get your piety, like a *pieta*, pose impossible to hold
for any length of time, that groaning dome, that rolling barrel belly.
It's made your heart dry and blacken like a martyr's relic
beneath the sweat sop arms of your buttoned up blouse.
I scour for postcards of marvellous birthing scenes,
Piero's *Madonne del parto* is my favourite. No shame.
A feverish neophyte strips without hesitation.
A *del parto*, even in times of turbulence, bonfires, chains.
The Oyster gleaming with Pearl behind the angels' curtains.

Jane Weir
Anna Magnani, eat with me, Templar Poetry

ON SIGHT

misjudging my weight from a brief eye up
the anaesthetist presents me with an impeccably terrible level
setting me paralysed but able to feel
my eyelid being slit open.

screens hover above me
relaying the performance of a cataract op next door.
the scrape of the spatula, the bite of staples,
six fingers pushing my eyeball into the socket
to check if the wound would bleed.

nurse sings along to the radio
until I squeeze her hand.
we had only just met,
and look what they've done.

just like the three boys who dared
the only girl to run
towards the wide mossy tree
then propelled a stick or rock or paving brick
to chase after her grinning skull.

knocked out momentarily, a patch of her head scalped
she waited till dark to show someone and ask:
will I die in the night?

Jen Calleja
Serious Justice, Test Centre

Flowers From The Dark

She is quiet,
With skin as tight as the wheeling crows:
She kneels over the dirt and grows
The roses.
Your lawn chair holds a pale absence;
A tulip dies, falls back against the fence,
And decomposes.

You watch her.
(And from her fair and unpolluted flesh)
The shadows on the windowsill – fresh
Violets
Break up the clean square of light,
And, thoughtless, obstruct the sight
Of her silence.

She grows the flowers
For you. From loam and wombs,
The pits of eyes and empty rooms,
From hipbones,
Harpoons, moons and crows: everything dark –
Seaweed, oil, the time around stars;
And olive stones.

Ashani Lewis
Wonder Competition, Tower Poetry

Angel 17

While in front of him the mountain of wreckage
rises towards the sky. It's the wreckage of what's
been developed, exploited, consumed or those things
waiting to be inspected and maybe consumed.
But why should this pulverised mess, pointing skywards,
be shaped like a giant ant hill? It suggests an idea of industry
and progress, even nostalgia for the great chain of being.
"I was the second link in the chain and you were the third."
said the angel to the man guarding the gate of the wrecker's
yard. "From the plants, grass and minerals, all the way up
to God, we once knew our place and our function. Then you
broke the chain, exchanging a hierarchy for a hill going
nowhere." The angel looked back at the hill and knew that
one day there would be nothing left to pile on top. And all
the histories, weary of their materialism, would come to an end.

Alan Price
Angels at the Edge, Tuba Press

What my daughter taught me

How to change a nappy in my sleep.
To get from doze to dressed in seven minutes flat.
That distance isn't always about miles.
To make a mean lasagne without meat.

That the angle on a dog's leg's not an elbow but a wrist.
That 'I love you' must be said.
Which exercises free a stiffened neck.
Not to hope for gratitude.

How to stack a dishwasher.
That for the middle-aged, red's preferable to buff.
To jog, heel hitting pavement first.
That sometimes love is not enough.

Gill Learner
Chill Factor, Two Rivers Press

Provenance

Somewhere in the swirl of paint
lies moisture captured from his breath,
some slight impression of his gaze,
the weight of hours in a draughty loft.

Collectors breathe the painter's dust,
observe as women stitch their silks
and sunlight falls on a chequered floor.
They want to own the artist's essence,
touching atoms, brushing fingers,
seeking to be part of him,
his fame illuminating theirs.

Goering, finding his Vermeer
was fake, was shocked, as if he'd just
discovered there is evil in the world.

Kathy Gee
Book of Bones, V. Press

How to Knit a Sheep

Start with the legs. It helps to
grab a hoof before casting on, or
he might kick you off. Hold the yarn
taut enough to test his strength,
loose enough to feel his flank quiver
as he bunches shanks to stretch the
ply, hoping it will fray. Loop and dip,
add sufficient stitches to keep his
interest, praise his beauty while
you unravel him, tug gently or he'll
slip your noose. Twist and roll, turn
and back again, keep your palm
against his side as you slide the pins
around about, each click a kiss,
each gartered purl a sweet low
riff to make him give it all, slough
that fleece in one soft piece
to flow from fingertips to floor.
Scoop it up and sniff warm oil
rising through his staple, the crop
he gives up now with grace. Keep
your face pressed to his curls,
breathe the heat and wax of him
behind his ears as hands move
faster as you near the end, his chest
bare and cold, your feet hot under
so much weight. Tie the ends off tight
before you let him go, your nose to his
in thanks only eskimos understand.

Di Slaney
Reward for Winter, Valley Press

Cigarettes on Grey Street

corner seem appropriate.
You're telling me you're a
redsmith for a contemporary
gallery and some northern
university or another, while
assuming me up and down.

I'm wearing a plastic red
mack and nude heels with
slack slingbacks lacking
any firm ankle support
but more than adept at
softly killing wet pavements.

Red hot tar's spread on my
soul, which you'll never
see, and my black silk scarf
is strangling me with a
permanent knot I just can't
get out with casual dexterity

and we're licking our tongues
on mendacity, treated like
a noun, personified to within
an inch of its life. Where will
we go tomorrow? Who will
we be? At the red-lit man

pack-of-cards pedestrians seem
happy to crash into the same
old routine of a rush hour's

matt grey sky and twilight
petrol fumes, pushing hectic
around before Dean Street.

Through the vision in your eyes
I can see you're approximately
years and years behind me, I
need breeze from the quayside,
feeling inclined to find my own
highlights, perfect timing or a

shot of some other metallic; without
looking back I step into the traffic.

Julie Hogg
Majuba Road, Vane Women Press

Mr and Mrs Death

He was always a few millimetres
under her skin, a parallel universe

the same shape as her shape.
She's a bowl of fruit decaying

in a speeded up video installation
collapses with his bruise inside.

His vase is a shaft of no light
her entrance a door opening inwards.

She rises up, to open to the beloved
a conjurer who swallows her own wand.

She sucks pomegranate seeds from his fingers
hopes her mother knows where she is

notices the lock
is choking on the key.

There's no window to look at the security lights from.
She can't see the dogs on the lawn.

Marion Tracy
Dreaming of Our Better Selves, Vanguard Editions

[**extract**]

emissaries of the snout.
The tradition of the dotted line:

admin.

Sentence to be shot
Sentence, to exile.
Sentence, silent meta
stasis of each camp.

On the basis of lists it's curtains
in the courtyard.
Jam
in the courtyard
Jam
at the gates.
Red in black at every entrance,
Judas holes in every wall you
Thought maybe those words you
Thought were yours but now they eat you
now they eat you now they
Bring you and they x you in
your faces dotted lines every time
& no not
even the dead are safe.

Frances Kruk
lo-fi frags in-progress, Veer Books

On a scale of nought to ten

Where ten equals *the depth and breadth and height*
and nought equals *why are you stalking me?*

Where nine equals *as long as we both shall live*
and one equals *I said no yesterday and I'm saying no today.*

And eight equals *fingers crossed, this one is different*
and two equals *it's not your fault, it's mine*

And seven equals *a dozen red roses, and "sorry" on the card*
and three equals *just don't take me for granted*

And six equals *I want to be with you all the time*
and four equals *we can't be together all the time*

And five equals *sometimes I do and sometimes I don't*
but stick around and it just might work –

how do you love me?

Ann Alexander
Old Things, Ward Wood Publishing

Beast

I shall *ride* you
BEAST!

Although you plunge me into abysses,
across the terrifying crevasses, towards *sheer precipices.*

I shall ride you
BEAST!

And when you try to throw me off, to trample me, and eat me,
I shall show you that you cannot beat me.

BEAST.
Wherever it is you take me,
though your fierce heart wants to consume me,
rake me into the ashes,
you shall *not* undo me;
You shall *not* unmake me.

BEAST.
On your broad back
I'll course the shadowed lands,
on your broad back one day I'll stand
and feel the wind run through me.
In quiet, sunlit pastures one fine day,

you'll be eating gently

from my hands.

IDF Andrew
Of the Deep, William Cornelius Harris Publishing

Painting the sea

A piano might just do it.
If it were possible of course
to get one out there
and if one knew
how to hit the notes
as if shoving and elbowing,
shouldering grit and
chucking it quite so untidily,
letting each note slide
into another
like small stones
bruising their backs
on water. Next the rasp
of bristles on paint.
This is a picture. In the picture
a small piano
is being eaten by the sea
while fragments
of what looks like paper
smudge the outline,
bounce and hop against the frame.

Carolyn Oulton
Accidental Fruit, Worple Press

Court

The cradled moon cauled in her own grimace
Is the stone hymn, young rocks face
glare through the paths of stars.
Stone light shatters her milky furnace
once angle tilts and what is to come?

Devon holm gnawed etchers bark by stone age tomb
William's son wounds seep into clay
Christ in clay offers his revelation
they carve and dig and still gape moonlight
in twigs they are put out to crow and hawk's nest

in the bridal bridles of marl day courts the flint
sparks married to cosmic blaze
married to fires blaze, reigns in fires to bit
yet calls home the jessy to his gobbet

hawk's talons churned a wraithed mist
of blood from thrushes vigilant song
air's cruel warder of each jailbird

breath short blue burned the ashes of words
and the perdital airs' rope's end
is in this steeleyed lung you echo from.

Colin Honnor
The Honest Ulsterman, Yew Tree Press

UK Poetry Publisher Listings

Please note that all listings, where possible, have been written by the publishers themselves. We apologies for any absences. If you represent a publisher not shown below, please email poetrybookfair@gmail.com to get listed for free. At time of going to press we counted 180 active UK poetry publishers.

13 Pages

- 13pp.wordpress.com | thirteenpages@gmail.com
- London | Founded 2011
- Editors: Will Harris & Richard Osmond
- Pamphlets, Anthologies
- Unsolicited submissions not currently accepted.

13 Pages values is poetry that's obviously not transparent. Craft and artifice – not in the sense of falseness, but rather a kind of irreducible, intricately well-made thoughtfulness by which images, concepts and everyday patterns of speech are made into original, effective, affective, aesthetically-pleasing forms. The poem isn't a window to be looked through – it's a finely-wrought reflective surface that can only be looked at.

A Midsummer Night's Press

- amidsummernightspress.com | amidsummernightspress@gmail.com
- New York, USA | Founded 2007
- Publisher: Lawrence Schimel
- Pamphlets, Single-Author Collections, Anthologies (including the work of UK-based poets)
- Anthology projects (announced on website when we are reading for one) are open to unsolicited submissions.

We publish in 4 areas: Fabula Rasa (poetry of myth & fairy tale), Body Language (LGBT voices), Sapphic Classics (reissued important lesbian feminist works), Periscope (poetry in translation by women poets).

Acumen Publications

- acumen-poetry.co.uk | patriciaoxley6@gmail.com
- Brixham, Devon | Founded 1985
- Editor: Patricia Oxley
- Pamphlets, *Acumen Literary Journal*
- Submissions welcome (see website for details).

Please see website for further information.

Agenda Poetry

- agendapoetry.co.uk | editor@agendapoetry.co.uk
- East Sussex | Founded 1959
- Editor: Patricia McCarthy
- Pamphlets, Single-Author Collections, *Agenda* (magazine)
- Submissions welcome only in specific reading windows (see website for details).

Agenda is a very highly regarded national/international journal, founded by William Cookson and Ezra Pound in 1959, and edited now by Patricia McCarthy. It promotes known, little known and new voices. It also encourages young poets by highlighting two or three each time in the journal and by featuring them, along with young artists, in the online Broadsheets (now up to No 27). An ongoing series, both in the printed journal and online, *Notes for Broadsheet Poets*, gives tips and inspiration for the writing of poetry, especially directed at young poets, students and their mentors. Poems and paintings are also featured in the online web supplements. The material on the website is archived by The Bodleian. Agenda believes in a poetry that matters, that is musical, that moves and communicates in a way that ordinary conversational words cannot. Essays and reviews are also published in the journal. Those wanting to submit their work are advised to subscribe to the journal first (easy to do online).

Alba Publishing

- albapublishing.com

Alba Publishing publishes poetry, haiku and tanka poetry and haibun collections and chapbooks by established writers in these genres. Founder and publisher Kim Richardson has worked in publishing for nearly 40 years and, as Alba Publishing, specializes in short-run editions, aiming to bring the highest standards of design and production to showcase writers' work.

Allardyce, Barnett, Publishers

- abar.net | ab@abar.net
- East Sussex | Founded 1980s
- Editor: Anthony Barnett
- Single-Author Collections, Books about Poetry, *Snow lit rev*
- Book submissions not accepted. Visit www.abar.net/snow.pdf for *Snow lit rev* submissions information.

Allardyce, Barnett, Publishers and imprint Allardyce Book ABP published the first collected editions of JH Prynne, Douglas Oliver, Veronica Forrest-Thomson, Andrew Crozier. Currently it publishes books of poetry and prose by Anthony Barnett, including music history. The review *Snow lit rev*, which appears approximately once a year, publishes prose, poetry, art, photography, music, film.

Anima Poetry Press

- animapoetry.uk
- West Sussex | Founded 2014
- Editor: Marcus Sly; Assistant Editor: Alyson Hallett
- Single-Author Collections, *Anima* (magazine)
- Submissions welcome only in specific reading windows (see website for details).

Anima publishes contemporary poetry which dares to question the materialist paradigm of western culture. We aim to offer the reader thoughtful and intelligent writing from perspectives beyond the everyday world of sense and reason. Poems of metaphysics, mythology and symbolism, of depth psychology or transcendence – all these and more are welcome in our pages.

Aquifer Books

- glasfrynproject.org.uk | aquiferbooks@gmail.com
- Powys, Wales | Founded 2014
- Editor: Lyndon Davies
- Single-Author Collections, Anthologies
- Unsolicited submissions not currently accepted.

Aquifer Books – a very new venture – publishes poetry collections but its remit includes writings in different genres by poets, including, for instance, diaries, novels, journals, reportage, critical and philosophical meditations, letters and so on. The bias is towards experimental work, and one of Aquifer's aims is to provide a publishing outlet for such writing being done on the Welsh scene, as well as further afield. As far as possible Aquifer works hand in glove with the author to create a product which seeks to celebrate the individual qualities of each particular publication, eschewing the notion of house-style.

Arachne Press

- arachnepress.com | cherry@arachnepress.com
- London | Founded 2012
- Editor: Cherry Potts
- Single-Author Collections, Anthologies, Fiction
- Submissions welcome only in specific reading windows (see website for details).

We have a particular interest in narrative poetry – either collections that tell a story across the poems, or long poems that have a narrative drive. We run live events including the Solstice Shorts Festival (21st December each year) in Greenwich, which has a strong poetry thread.

Arc Publications

- arcpublications.co.uk
- Lancashire | 1969
- Editors: Tony Ward, Angela Jarman

Arc publishes contemporary poetry from new and established writers from the UK and abroad, specialising in the work of international poets writing in English and the work of overseas poets in translation. This year their poets have included Josep Lluís Aguiló, Linda France, Hugo Mujica and many more.

Augur Press

- augurpress.com
- Midlothian | founded 2004
- Proprietor: Mirabelle Maslin
- Chapbooks
- Can sometimes look at submissions.

Augur Press publishes books that enable the reader to reflect, and to look beyond or behind that which is immediately apparent.

Awen Publications

- awenpublications.co.uk | publisher@awenpublications.co.uk
- Stroud, Gloucestershire | Founded 2003
- Publisher: Anthony Nanson; Founder: Kevan Manwaring
- Pamphlets, Single-Author Collections, Anthologies, Books about Poetry, Fiction, Literary Non-Fiction
- Unsolicited submissions not currently accepted.

Awen's mission is to publish works of poetry, fiction, and literary non-fiction that match quality of writing with an engagement with the world. We believe in the need to bring spiritual and ecological values into contemporary writing. More about our vision can be found in *An Ecobardic Manifesto: A Vision for the Arts in a Time of Environmental Crisis*: visit our website for more information.

Banipal Publishing

- banipal.co.uk | margaret@banipal.co.uk
- London | Founded 1998

- Publisher: Margaret Obank; Editor: Samuel Shimon
- Books about Poetry, *Banipal Magazine*
- Submissions welcome (see website for details).

Banipal Magazine, showcasing the best of today's literary voices from all over the Arab world in English translation, is a vital bridge presenting established and emerging Arab writers through poems, short stories or excerpts of novels, free from cultural stereotypes and making a unique contribution to world literature and intercultural dialogue. Includes interviews with authors, publishers and translators, book reviews and photo-reports of literary events.

Bare Fiction

- barefictionmagazine.co.uk
- Shropshire | Founded 2013
- Pamphlets, Single-Author Collections, *Bare Fiction* (magazine)
- Submissions welcome (see website for details).

Bare Fiction was set up to promote new writing in all forms through performance, digital representation and publication. They recently published work by Bare Fiction Debut Poetry Collection Competition winners Jo Duffy, Peter Wallis and Annette C. Boehm.

Barque Press

- barquepress.com
- London & Sussex | Founded 1995
- Books, Chapbooks, *Quid* (magazine)
- Editors: Andrea Brady and Keston Sutherland

- Submissions only currently accepted for *Quid* (see website for details).

Barque Press has published over 40 chapbooks and six perfect bound books, as well as four CD-Rs, which include spoken word performances by a variety of artists alongside improvisational music. These are an offshoot of *Quid* magazine, which regularly includes poetry, prose, and critical essays. Formerly print-based, the magazine is now distributed gratis as Adobe Acrobat files from our website.

Beautiful Dragons

- beautiful-dragons.com

Beautiful Dragons Press is an entirely collaborative, not-for-profit poetry press where the dragons of invention meet the fires of association and magic occurs. Or something very close. They have collaborated with many poets, including Angela Topping and Anna Crowe.

Black & BLUE

- blackbluewriting.com
- Manchester | Founded 2011

Black & BLUE is a writing collective, making print anthologies of contemporary creative writing. Their latest anthology was *Revolution*, which included poems by Sarah Chapman, Toby Martinez de las Rivas and Julia Tolo. They produce political poetic pamphlets, organise exhibitions for text art and write about literature, art and theory.

Blart Books

- blartmagazine.jimdo.com | blartmagazine@gmail.com
- Romney Marsh | Founded 2011
- Editors: Lucy Harvesy Clark, Stephen Emmerson
- Single-Author Collections
- Submissions welcome (see website for details).

Publishing non academic, innovative poetry.

Bloodaxe Books

- bloodaxebooks.com
- Hexham | Founded 1978
- Editor: Neil Astley; Executive Chair: Simon Thirsk
- Single-Author Collections, Anthologies, Selecteds and Collecteds
- Submissions welcome (see website for details).

Bloodaxe has revolutionised poetry publishing in Britain over four decades. Internationally renowned for quality in literature and excellence in book design, our authors and books have won virtually every major literary award given to poetry, from the T.S. Eliot Prize and Pulitzer to the Queen's Gold Medal for Poetry and the Nobel Prize. And books like the *Staying Alive* trilogy have broken new ground by opening up contemporary poetry to many thousands of new readers. Bloodaxe's latest list again reflects the innovative, international and diverse range of our poetry publishing, including four books of poetry in translation and four anthologies along with R.S. Thomas's previously unknown poems on modern art and an unexpected late collection from Roy Fisher. As well as many writers from Britain and Ireland, this year's programme includes poets from the US, Australia, Jamaica, Guyana, Malawi, Spain, Sri Lanka and Sudan.

Book Works

- bookworks.org.uk

Book Works are a small arts publisher. They recently published Holly Pester's *Go to reception and ask for sara in red felt tip.*

British Haiku Society

- britishhaikusociety.org.uk
- UK | Founded 1991
- Editor: David Serjeant
- Pamphlets, Anthologies, Books about Poetry, *Blithe Spirit*
- Submissions welcome (see website for details).

We publish haiku and related forms (tanka, haibun and renku), articles and book reviews.

Burning Eye Books

- burningeyebooks.co.uk | infodata@burningeye.co.uk
- Somerset | Founded 2012
- Editors: Clive Birnie, Jenn Hart
- Pamphlets, Single-Author Collections, Anthologies
- Submissions welcome only in specific reading windows (see website for details).

Burning Eye Books is a small independent publishers based in the South West. We specialise in promoting emerging and established spoken word artists with the aim to dispel the assumption that performance poetry does not transfer well to page. We like to explore west of centre to seek out the experimental, the political and the outspoken.

Calder Valley Poetry

- caldervalleypoetry.com | caldervalleypoetry@yahoo.com
- West Yorkshire | Founded 2016
- Editor: Bob Horne
- Pamphlets
- Unsolicited submissions not currently accepted.

Calder Valley Poetry is a small press which commenced publication in January 2016 with John Foggin's collection *Outlaws and Fallen Angels*. It is intended to produce pamphlets by the many fine poets living alongside what was once referred to as Yorkshire's 'river of industry'. These are writers who have a casual, even indifferent, attitude to publication. Coaxing, threats, blackmail will be employed, where appropriate, in order to provide them with the wider readership they deserve. However, far from being parochial, Calder Valley Poetry will also pursue the poets of Kirklees and the Colne valley. And once across the watershed, who can tell where, in years to come, its grasp might reach? Or what's a small press for?

Candlestick Press

- candlestickpress.co.uk
- Nottingham | Founded 2008

Candlestick Press publishes poetry pamphlets aimed equally at people familiar with poetry and those who are not. Their pamphlets make an ideal alternative to a mainstream greetings card. They have matching envelopes and bookmarks left blank for your message and are excellent for a bedtime read.

Canongate

- canongate.tv
- Edinburgh | Founded 1973

Canongate is an independent publisher and founding member of the Independent Alliance. Their poetry list includes poets as diverse as Anna Akhmatova, Lemn Sissay and Tim Key.

Carcanet Press

- carcanet.co.uk | info@carcanet.co.uk
- Manchester | Founded 1969
- Managing Director: Michael Schmidt; Managing Editor: Luke Allan
- Single-Author Collections, Anthologies, Books about Poetry, Lives and Letters, Literary Criticism, Biography, *PN Review*
- Submissions welcome (see website for details).

Based in Manchester, Carcanet Press is one of the outstanding independent literary publishers of our time. Now in its fifth decade, Carcanet publishes the most comprehensive and diverse list available of modern and classic poetry in English and in translation, as well as a range of inventive fiction, Lives and Letters and literary criticism. In 2015, Carcanet received the Independent Publishers Guild Alison Morrison Diversity Award, was shortlisted for the IPG Trade Publisher of the Year Award, and shortlisted for the Bookseller Independent Publisher of the Year Award.

CB editions

- cbeditions.com | info@cbeditions.com
- London | 2007
- Editor: Charles Boyle
- Single-Author Collections, *Sonofabook* (magazine)
- Unsolicited submissions not currently accepted.

CBe publishes US poets (D. Nurkse, Dan O'Brien, Matthew Siegel) and poetry in translation (Apollinaire, Giannuzzi, Ponge) as well as contemporary British poets. Many of the books have a strong formal unity, being continuous verse narratives or linked sequences.

Chatto & Windus

- penguinrandomhouse.co.uk
- London | Founded 1855
- Editor: Parisa Ebrahimi

Chatto & Windus is the oldest continuous imprint of Penguin Random House UK. Authors in its newly reinvigorated poetry ouput include Helen Mort, Liz Berry and Sarah Howe.

Cinnamon Press

- cinnamonpress.com
- Gwynedd, North Wales | Founded 2005

Cinnamon Press is a small, independent publisher run by a family team. They select books they feel passionate about and concentrate on a small list of titles. The press also incorporates Liquorice Fish Books.

Circaidy Gregory Press

- circaidygregory.co.uk | info@circaidygregory.co.uk
- Hastings | Founded 2006
- Editor: Kay Green
- Single-Author Collections, Novels, Plays, Specialist Non-Fiction
- Unsolicited submissions not currently accepted.

Gives preference to titles by winners and shortlisted authors from Earlyworks Press writing competitions. Occasionally accepts propositions from elsewhere – mostly novels or poetry.

Clinic Publishing

- clinicpresents.com | clinicpresents@gmail.com
- London | Founded 2009
- Editors: Andrew Parkes, Rachael Allen, Sam Buchan-Watts, Sean Roy Parker
- Pamphlets, Anthologies
- Submissions welcome (see website for details).

Clinic began in 2009 as a small poetry workshop in a Southeast London Millwall pub before moving into live events and publishing anthologies, pamphlets and one-off commissioned publications. Our aim has always been to bring about new collaborations and conversations between artists and poets, alongside providing a nurturing platform for writers in the early stages of their careers. We recently published a collection of newly-commissioned work inspired by The Simpsons and pamphlets from Chloe Stopa-Hunt and Edwina Attlee.

Clutag Press

- clutagpress.com
- Oxfordshire | Founded in 2000
- Unsolicited submissions not currently accepted.

Clutag is a small independent press. It publishes poetry and memoir, and the magazine *Archipelago*. Previous pamphlets have included Seamus Heaney and Anne Stevenson.

Comma Press

- commapress.co.uk | commatranslation@yahoo.co.uk
- Manchester | Founded 2004
- Editor: Ra Page; Digital Editor: Jim Hinks
- Single-Author Collections, Anthologies
- Submissions welcome (see website for details).

Comma Press is a not-for-profit publishing initiative dedicated to promoting new writing, genre breaking texts, and just really good reads. It is committed to a spirit of risk-taking and challenging publishing, free of the commercial pressures on mainstream houses.

Corbel Stone Press

- corbelstonepress.com | corbelstonepress@yahoo.co.uk
- Fife | Founded 2009
- Editors: Autumn Richardson & Richard Skelton
- Pamphlets, Single-Author Collections, Music, Art Editions, *Reliquiae* (magazine)
- Submissions welcome only in specific reading windows (see website for details).

Corbel Stone Press is the small press of Autumn Richardson & Richard Skelton. We publish music, art and writing informed by landscape and nature. Our particular areas of interest are ecology, anthropology, folklore, animism and other-than-human consciousness.

Corrupt Press

- corruptpress.net | corrupt.press@hotmail.com
- Luxembourg | Founded 2011
- Editor: Dylan Harris
- Pamphlets, Single-Author Collections (including the work of UK-based poets)
- Submissions welcome only in specific reading windows (see website for details).

Corrupt Press is excited by the impact of internationalisation on English language poetry. Poets whose mother tongues don't include English, or who write from non-Anglophone cultures, are of particular interest. We stole our name from the newspaper industry, but are now ashamed to admit they've completely out-corrupted us.

Crater Press

- craterpress.co.uk
- London & Brighton | Founded 2009
- Unsolicited submissions not currently accepted.

The Crater Press publish, primarily through letterpress, distinctive pamphlets of innovative British poetry.

Critical Documents

- plantarchy.us
- London | Founded 2005
- Editor: Justin Katko

Critical Documents have published pamphlets and criticism by writers including JH Prynne, Tom Raworth and Sara Crangle.

Cultured Llama

- culturedllama.co.uk
- Kent | Founded 2011
- Editors: Bob Carling, Maria C. McCarthy
- Single-Author Collections, Short fiction and Curious Things
- Submissions welcome only in specific reading windows (see website for details).

Cultured Llama publishes collections of poetry, short fiction and Curious Things – cultural non-fiction, such as *The Ecology of Everyday Things* by Mark Everard. In 2016, Cultured Llama celebrates five years of independent publishing with its 27th publication: *There Are No Foreign Lands*, a debut poetry collection by Mark Holihan.

Dempsey & Windle

- dempseyandwindle.co.uk | janawindle@gmail.com
- Guildford | Founded 2010
- Editor: Janice Windle; Assistant Editor: Dónall Dempsey
- Pamphlets, Single-Author Collections, Anthologies
- Unsolicited submissions not currently accepted.

Dempsey & Windle publish poetry that they enjoy reading or hearing performed. Accessibility, honesty and a flair for original imagery are more important to them than strict forms. They offer writers of any age and every genre a chance to develop their work by providing a platform and an audience, both on the page and on the spoken word stage. Dempsey & Windle's anthologies are based on the monthly spoken word events they host in Guildford, where they showcase poets from all over Britain, and on their annual poetry competition. Poets worth individual collections edited by Janice Windle are selected through the competition, and offered publication. Humour and narrative, social comment and lyrical poems are equally welcomed in submissions and in performance. Above all, Dónall Dempsey and Janice Windle value genuine feeling communicated by any poetic means, and want to promote confidence and quality among new and more experienced writers.

Dock Road Press

- facebook.com/dockroadpress
- Liverpool | Founded 2016
- Pamphlets

Dock Road Press have published pamphlets by Nathan Walker, Sarah Crewe, Mark Greenwood, Cathy Butterworth and Paul Tarpey. We focus on experimental poetry:performance writing.

Earlyworks Press

- earlyworkspress.co.uk
- services@earlyworkspress.co.uk
- Hastings | Founded 2005

- Editor: Kay Green
- Collaborations, Anthologies, Local Interest Titles

Most titles by winners and shortlisted authors of Earlyworks Press competitions or club projects. Founded by a group of writers and artists to runs events, workshops and collaborative publishing projects. Membership, now centred on a private online forum, was built through international writing competitions, inviting authors to join club and/or projects.

Egg Box

- eggboxpublishing.com
- Norfolk | Founded 2002
- Editor: Nathan Hamilton

Egg Box has published anthologies of work by UEA students, as well as work by poets including Sam Riviere and Tom Warner.

The Emma Press

- theemmapress.com | queries@theemmapress.com
- Birmingham | Founded 2012
- Editor: Rachel Piercey; Publisher: Emma Wright
- Pamphlets, Anthologies, Single-Author Collections for Children
- Submissions welcome only in specific reading windows (see website for details).

The Emma Press is an independent poetry publisher run by Emma Wright and dedicated to producing beautiful, thought-provoking books. It publishes themed anthologies, single-author pamphlets and books for children, all printed on nice paper and often illustrated. The Emma Press was shortlisted for the Michael Marks Award for Poetry Pamphlet Publishers in both 2014 and 2015, and Emma Press pamphlets have won the Poetry Book Society Pamphlet Choice award and the Saboteur Award for Best Collaborative Work. The Emma Press is keen on making poetry welcoming and accessible, so they run lots of events and workshops. In 2015 they received a grant from Arts Council England to travel around the country with *Myths and Monsters*, a tour of poetry readings and workshops aimed at children aged 8+. They are often on the lookout for new writing, and run regular calls for submissions to their themed poetry anthologies and poetry pamphlet series.

Enitharmon Press

- enitharmon.co.uk | info@enitharmon.co.uk
- London | Founded 1967
- Directors: Stephen Stuart-Smith, Isabel Brittain
- Pamphlets, Single-Author Collections, Anthologies, Books about Poetry
- Unsolicited submissions not currently accepted.

Enitharmon was founded in 1967 and specialises in publishing poetry, artists' books and limited edition books and prints. It is recognised for its high standards of production and editorial care. Writers and artists associated with Enitharmon are: Simon Armitage, Samuel Beckett, Peter Blake, Jim Dine, Maureen Duffy, Seamus Heaney, David Hockney, Ted Hughes, Gilbert & George, Michael Longley, Paul Muldoon, Hughie O'Donoghue, Harold Pinter, Kathleen Raine, and Paula Rego. Enitharmon is a creation of William Blake. She is a muse of poetry and painting, representing spiritual beauty and inspiration. The Enitharmon logo derives from a Blake woodcut.

erbacce-press

- erbacce-press.webeden.co.uk
- Liverpool

A book and chapbook press that grew out of *erbacce* magazine.

Equinox Press

- davidcobb.co.uk
- Essex | Founded 1991

Active since 1991, promoting short forms.

Equipage Press

- equipagepress.weebly.com
- Cambridge
- Editor: Rod Mengham

Equipage Press began following the journal *equofinality*, edited by Rod Mengham and John Wilkinson. Publications in print include work by Simon Jarvis, John Kinsella, Barry MacSweeney, Peter Riley and Keston Sutherland.

Etruscan Books

- llpp.ms11.net/etruscan/index.html | etruscanpublishing@gmail.com
- Hastings | Founded 1996
- Editor: Nicholas Johnson
- Single-Author Collections
- Unsolicited submissions not currently accepted.

Etruscan Books is twenty years young, and has published concrete, Gaelic and modernist poetry with an ear for the lyric and the made up word. The books are carefully edited, and sewn, often with artist writer film maker collaborations. These have included James Ravilious, Basil King, Colin Sackett, Patrick Caulfield, the teenage Nicholas Dunbar, Rebecca E. Marshall, Sarah Simblett and Brigid McLeer. etruscan books are book makers, rather than orthodox poetry publishers. Many of their books are sold at the London Review of Books Bookshop, and Edinburgh's Word Power.

Exiled Writers Ink

- exiledwriters.co.uk | jennifer@exiledwriters.fsnet.co.uk
- London | Founded 2000
- *Exiled Ink Magazine* (online only at present), Pamphlets

Exiled Writers Ink specialises in work by refugee, migrant and exiled writers only.

Eyewear Publishing

- eyewearpublishing.com
- London | Founded 2012
- Editor: Todd Swift; Senior Poetry Editor: Kelly Davio; Editor: Oliver Jones
- Pamphlets, Single-Author Collections, Anthologies, Books about Poetry
- Submissions welcome (see website for details).

Eyewear Publishing is a new independent press, passionate about producing beautifully designed, fascinating books that remain affordable. Based in London, we celebrate the best writing in English from the UK and overseas. We bring readers a varied list that is full of different voices and styles, kept coherent by our dedication to presenting writers of the highest quality. Through our annual Melita Hume Poetry Prize we discover, support and develop exciting new poets, while also taking great pleasure in working with writers at all stages of their careers.We have been publishing poetry and prose since 2012. In an unstable climate for small press publishing we have a variety of financial strategies that allow us to continue to publish the very best writing and to ensure our long term success.

Faber & Faber

- faber.co.uk | members@faber.co.uk
- London | 1929
- Editor: Matthew Hollis
- Pamphlets, Single-Author Collections, Anthologies, Books about Poetry
- Submissions welcome (see website for details).

Faber & Faber remains one of the last of the great independent publishing houses in London. Established as a firm in 1929, and publishing many of the greats of the twentieth century, including Robert Lowell, Ted Hughes, Sylvia Plath, W. S. Graham, Marianne Moore, Philip Larkin and Seamus Heaney, Faber is committed to its strong frontlist alongside the depth of its backlist, and to remaining at the heart of poetry publishing.

Face Press

- [not currently online] | ijaheames@gmail.com
- Oxford, Cambridge, London | Founded 2009

- Editor: Ian Heames
- Pamphlets, Single-Author Collections, Books about Poetry, Broadsides, *No Prizes* (magazine)
- Unsolicited submissions not currently accepted.

Publisher of contemporary poetry. Risograph, letterpress, ink jet, colour copier, etc.

Fair Acre Press

- fairacrepress.co.uk
- Shropshire | Founded 2011
- Editor: Nadia Kingsley
- Pamphlets, Anthologies, Wildlife Photography, Poetry for Children, A Novel (we don't like to be pigeon-holed)
- Unsolicited submissions not currently accepted.

Fair Acre Press publish beautiful books and pamphlets. They don't like to be pigeon-holed: in 2016 they have published a literary, working-class novel, a full colour wildlife photography book, a poetry book for children, and their two poetry pamphlet competition winners, judged by Jonathan Edwards. Their output is small as they spend a lot of time on getting the book right, and helping it once its out in the world. This year's reviews and awards show they must be doing something right.

Fine Press Poetry

- finepresspoetry.com | andrewmoorhouse@me.com
- Rochdale, Lancs. | Founded 2013
- Editor: Andrew Moorhouse,
- Single-Author Collections
- Unsolicited submissions not currently accepted.

Working with established poets (Armitage, Longley, Motion) they publish beautiful letterpress printed, hardbound, illustrated books with the aim of living up to Updike's assertion that 'a book is beautiful in its relation to the human hand, to the human eye, to the human brain, and to the human spirit'.

Five Leaves Publications / Five Leaves Bookshop

- fiveleaves.co.uk | www.fiveleavesbookshop.co.uk | bookshop@fiveleaves.co.uk
- Nottingham | Founded 1995 (Publications), 2013 (Bookshop)
- Editor: Ross Bradshaw
- Pamphlets, Single-Author Collections, Anthologies
- Unsolicited submissions not currently accepted.

Five Leaves started life as a publisher, not solely of poetry. We now publish about ten books a year, one or two being poetry. The Bookshop has the biggest contemporary poetry section in the East Midlands and regularly hosts poetry readings and talks about poetry.

Flapjack Press

- flapjackpress.co.uk
- Salford, Gtr Manchester | Founded 2008
- Editor: Paul Neads
- Single-Author Collections
- Unsolicited submissions not currently accepted.

Flapjack Press: exploring the synergy between performance and the page. An independent publisher of north-west performance poetry and poetry theatre.

Flarestack Poets

- flarestackpoets.co.uk | flarestackpoets@gmail.com
- Birmingham | Founded 2009
- Editors: Jacqui Rowe, Meredith Andrea
- Pamphlets
- Submissions welcome only in specific reading windows (see website for details).

Flarestack Poets sees the pamphlet as a poetic form in itself, which Flarestack Poets' titles have explored and developed in different ways, through themes, voices, moods or in poems that play off each other more subtly. Instantly recognisable from their striking and range of cover colours, Flarestack Poets pamphlets are small, affordable works of art, beautifully produced, with meticulous attention to typesetting. The press has twice published the Pamphlet of the Year at the Michael Marks Awards, and in 2013 was Publisher of the Year.

flipped eye publishing

- flippedeye.net
- UK | Founded 2001
- Pamphlets, Single-Author Collections, Anthologies
- Submissions welcome via Submittable

flipped eye publishing's editorial focus is on work that is clear and true rather than exhibitionist. However, it is not averse to publishing work that might be considered experimental. Founded in 2001, flipped eye publishing has won or been shortlisted for awards from the PBS, IPG and Michael Marks Awards and has featured in most major publications worldwide, including The Guardian, New York Times, Independent on Sunday, Le Monde and Le Figaro.

Freight Books

- freightbooks.co.uk | info@freightbooks.co.uk
- Glasgow | Founded 2011
- Publisher: Adrian Searle
- Single-Author Collections, Anthologies, Books about Poetry, *Gutter* (magazine)
- Submissions welcome only in specific reading windows (see website for details).

Freight Books is a leading independent publisher, specialising in fiction, poetry, short stories and general non-fiction books for an English-speaking readership. Awarded Publisher of the Year by the Saltire Society in 2015, poetry books published by Freight have been shortlisted for the Forward Prize for Best First Collection, the Fenton Aldeburgh First Collection award, the Seamus Heaney Centre for Poetry Prize and others, and our poets include Harry Giles and Jim Carruth. Freight Books publishes *Gutter*, the magazine of new Scottish writing.

The Frogmore Press

- frogmorepress.co.uk | frogmorepress@gmail.com
- East Sussex | Founded 1983
- Editor: Dr Alexandra Loske; *The Frogmore Papers* Editor: Jeremy Page
- Pamphlets, Single-Author Collections, Anthologies, Life Writing, *The Frogmore Papers* (magazine)
- Unsolicited submissions not currently accepted.

The Frogmore Press was founded in Folkestone in 1983. In addition to the bi-annual literary journal *The Frogmore Papers*, it also publishes the online poetry magazine *morphrog* ('Poetry in the Extreme'). The Press has published individual collections by numerous poets, including Brian Aldiss, Clare Best, Robert Etty, Giles Goodland, Sophie Hannah, Geoffrey Holloway, Matthew Mead, Marita Over, Catherine Smith and Michael Swan, and several anthologies, of which the most recent have been *Languages of Colour* (2012, edited by Alexandra Loske) and *Poems from the Old Hill* (2012, edited by Jeremy Page).

Galley Beggar Press

- galleybeggar.co.uk
- Norwich | Founded 2012

Galley Beggar Press was set up to act as a sponsor to writers who have struggled to either find or retain a publisher, and (most importantly) whose writing shows great ambition and literary merit. Please visit the website for more details.

Gatehouse Press

- gatehousepress.com | admin@gatehousepress.com
- Norwich | Founded 2006
- Managing Director: Andrew McDonnell; Poetry Editor / Director: Meirion Jordan
- Pamphlets, Single-Author Collections, Anthologies, *Lighthouse* (magazine)
- Submissions welcome (see website for details).

Gatehouse's mission is to support new writers, primarily through publishing poetry and short stories. We aim to provide a platform both for new writers from across the UK, and for established writers who are seeking to develop innovative new projects. Our intention is to expand the range of avenues available to new writers through publishing exciting new work, both through our quarterly journal, Lighthouse, and our poetry and short fiction pamphlet series. Design is important to us too – we believe a book or a journal should be a beautiful thing that a reader will be pleased to have on their shelf. In 2015 *Lighthouse* won the Saboteur Award for best magazine, and in 2016 "Fool's World Tarot" by Helen Ivory and artist Tome de Freston won the Saboteur award for best collaboration.We are a not-for-profit company. Gatehouse Press directors and editors contribute their time and effort on a voluntary basis.

Gomer Press

- gomer.co.uk
- Llandysul, Wales | Founded 1892

Gomer Press is both a thriving printing company and the largest publishing house in Wales. Every year, they publish over 120 titles, specializing in books with a distinctive Welsh identity.

Graft Poetry

- graftpoetry.co.uk
- West Yorkshire | Founded 2008

Graft Poetry's philosophy is simple: the very best in contemporary poetry at affordable prices, publishing poets who deserve to be better known in book form.

Green Bottle Press

- greenbottlepress.com | jennifer@greenbottlepress.com
- London | Founded 2014
- Editor: Jennifer Grigg
- Pamphlets, Single-Author Collections
- Submissions welcome (see website for details).

Founded to publish first pamphlets and first collections by poets writing in English who have good track records of publication in some of the well-known journals and/or are prize-winners or have been shortlisted in competitions. Their books are beautifully produced and designed. They currently publish about four poets a year, but this may increase. They are interested in poetry that surprises them with unusual language and imagery.

Grey Hen Press

- greyhenpress.com | info@greyhenpress.com
- Kendal, Cumbria | Founded 2007
- Editor & Director: Joy Howard
- Anthologies, Chapbooks (under Hen Run imprint)
- Unsolicited submissions not currently accepted.

Grey Hen is a poetry press designed to showcase the work of older women by producing themed anthologies. Contributors include well-known and established poets alongside those whose work deserves to be better known, but who may be struggling to build up a publishing CV. It gets harder as you get older, especially for women, to get that first publication. Every effort is made to put on readings across the UK, to give all contributing poets a chance to participate. An annual competition for women over 60 brings a great response, and has brought new contributors to the anthologies. Grey Hen poets now number over 140.

GUG Press

- gugpress.com
- London | Founded 2016
- Editor: Francis Byrne
- Pamphlets, Single-Author Collections, Anthologies
- Submissions welcome (see website for details).

GUG Press is an independent press putting out fresh, playful writing. We publish new work with a focus on the experimental and conceptual that explores the plasticity of language and the antics of unordinary meaning. Our pamphlets and collections are conceptually frisky and offer challenging, progressive entries into the unknowns of extreme meaning, whilst the annual anthology we publish celebrates the hugely creative output of London's poetry scene.

Happen*Stance* Press

- happenstancepress.com | nell@happenstancepress.com
- Fife | Founded 2005
- Editor: Helena Nelson
- Pamphlets, Single-Author Collections, Anthologies, Books about Poetry, recently a Memoir
- Submissions welcome only in specific reading windows (see website for details).

We look for work that's startling and clear. We like poems that welcome the reader in (which is not to say they'll be easy or predictable). The editor/poet relationship is pivotal because the approach here is hands-on, working with each poet – whether debut or established writer – to make the work as good as it can be. So there's a lot of interaction, and much checking, obsessing, redrafting and agonising. We thrive on self-doubt.

Hazard Press

- hazardpress.co.uk | jh_dixon@hotmail.com
- Cardiff | Founded 2010
- Editor: Jeremy Dixon
- Poetic Artist's Books
- Unsolicited submissions not currently accepted.

Hazard Press was founded in 2010 specifically to publish the Artist's Books written, designed and made by Jeremy Dixon. The limited-edition books feature a combination of poetry, photography and different print processes such as letterpress and laser-printing. The books have rather unexpectedly formed an on-going project of autobiography based on language, memory, queerness, music, images, and a delight in the accidental forms and diversions that the journey of making a book can take. The subjects of Hazard Press books are very diverse, encompassing pilgrimages to the graves of the poets Emily Dickinson and Dylan Thomas, the songs of Shirley Bassey and Bobbie Gentry, the gay subculture of Chicago, and the weaving of vintage stamps into strips of paper. Hazard Press will occasionally publish the work of other poets, such as a micro-book for the tour of *Gelynion: The Enemies Project in Wales*, but collaborations are infrequent and dependent on circumstance.

Hearing Eye

- hearingeye.org | hearing_eye@torriano.org
- London | Founded 1987
- Editors: Susan Johns, Emily Johns
- Pamphlets, Single-Author Collections, Anthologies, Books about Poetry, Posters
- Unsolicited submissions not currently accepted.

Hearing Eye was established by John Rety and Susan Johns in 1987. Since then we have published over 200 books and pamphlets, from haiku to epic poems, by new and established poets. It is based at Torriano Meeting House in London which hosts weekly readings with a wide range of readers, including Stephen Watts, Timothy Adès, Les Murray and Mimi Khalvati. Many Hearing Eye authors are poets who have read at the Meeting House.

Henningham Family Press

- henninghamfamilypress.co.uk | david@henninghamfamilypress.co.uk
- London | Founded 2006
- Founders: David Henningham, Ping Henningham
- Anthologies, Essays and Fiction, Single-Author Collections

HFP encompasses the art, writing and Performance Publishing of David and Ping Henningham, and their collaborations with authors and artists on specialist printing and binding projects. They derive multiple books, prints and performances from their writing, often with live screenprinting. In partnership with museums and institutions, artists and authors, they create deluxe and idiosyncratic small-run publications often as a legacy for events, specialising in book design, fine printing and binding.

Hercules Editions

- herculeseditions.com | tamar@herculeseditions.com
- London | Founded 2012
- Editor: Tamar Yoseloff
- Pamphlets
- Submissions welcome (see website for details).

Hercules Editions is an independent press founded in 2012 by poet Tamar Yoseloff and art editor and designer Vici MacDonald. The focus is on combining poetry and prose with art and archival material to create beautiful small books and prints. Their debut publication, *Formerly*, was shortlisted for the Ted Hughes Award. The press is based near the site of artist-poet William Blake's home and printing works in Hercules Road, Lambeth, which inspired the name. Authors include Sue Rose, Claire Crowther, Hannah Lowe, and most recently, Sean O'Brien, whose new chapbook, *Hammersmith*, is a creative reimagining of the west London area through poetry and photographs.

Hi Zero

- hizeroreadings.tumblr.com
- Brighton

As well as their publications, Hi Zero is also a series of avant-garde experimental poetry readings and performances which is sponsored by the Centre for Modernist Studies in Brighton.

Holland Park Press

- hollandparkpress.co.uk | enquiries@hollandparkpress.co.uk
- London | Founded 2009

- Publisher: Bernadette Jansen op de Haar; Editor: Arnold Jansen op de Haar
- Single-Author Collections, Anthologies, Novels, Novellas, Short Story Collections
- Submissions welcome (see website for details).

A unique publishing initiative, aiming to promote poetry and literary fiction, and discover new writers. It specializes in contemporary English fiction and poetry, and translations of Dutch classics. It also gives contemporary Dutch writers the opportunity to be published in Dutch and English.

Hurst Street Press

- hurststreetpress.co.uk | shoshana@hurststreetpress.co.uk
- Oxford | Founded 2015
- Editors: Shoshana Kessler, Beth Sparks
- Pamphlets, Single-Author Collections, *IRIS: A Collaboration*
- Submissions welcome only in specific reading windows (see website for details).

Hurst Street Press is an independent printing press and publishing house. Its driving aim is to disseminate original works of literature and art using traditional techniques of production. It employs a combination of letterpress and risograph-printing, hand-stitching and binding to make each copy singular.

If a Leaf Falls Press

- samriviere.com/index.php?/together/if-a-leaf-falls-press
- Edinburgh | Founded 2015
- Editor: Sam Riviere
- Pamphlets

- Submissions welcome (see website for details).

If a Leaf Falls Press publishes very limited edition poetry with an emphasis on appropriative and arbitrary writing processes.

if p then q

- ifpthenq.co.uk | mail@ifpthenq.co.uk
- Manchester | 2008
- Editor: James Davies
- Single-Author Collections, Poetry Objects
- Unsolicited submissions not currently accepted.

if p then q is a publisher of experimental poetry with a particular interest in Minimalist and Conceptual poetry. Authors include P. Inman, Tom Jenks and Holly Pester.

Indigo Dreams Publishing

- indigodreams.co.uk | publishing@indigodreams.co.uk
- Devon | Founded 2004
- Editors: Ronnie Goodyer, Dawn Bauling
- Pamphlets, Single-Author Collections, Anthologies, *Reach Poetry, The Dawntreader, Sarasvati*
- Submissions welcome (see website for details).

We are an independent poetry publisher based in rural Devon. We publish around 40 collections/pamphlets each year together with total of 20 magazine issues. Indigo also runs an annual publishing prize in honour of poet/publisher Geoff Stevens and a pamphlet competition. We are known for our excellent author working relationship and our 'pleasure not pressure' ethos. Both new and established poets are welcome and in 2015 we won the

Ted Slade Award in recognition of our services to poetry. We were runners-up in the Most Innovative Publisher category and winner of the Best Pamphlet category at 2016 Saboteur Awards. Poets are selected on our personal taste with time capacity the only restriction. In addition we have paid over £10,500 in prize money to assist our poets. Our website shows the opportunities available and support is always appreciated!

Inkandescent

- inkandescent.co.uk | justin@inkandescent.co.uk
- London | Founded 2016
- Editor: Justin David
- Pamphlets, Books about Poetry, Single Author Collections
- Unsolicited submissions not currently accepted.

Inkandescent publications fuse literature and photography.

Iron Press

- ironpress.co.uk/poetry.html
- North Shields | Founded 1973

As publishers become more corporate, global and boring, IRON Press champions new quality writing as it has done since 1973. IRON runs events and launches; it also thinks literature is both serious and fun. IRON Press editor Peter Mortimer chooses his words carefully in his latest entry on the Inpress blog. No formula writing here – we spurn literary competitions and prizes, marketing junkets, vacuous works by overhyped minor celebrities, or other books whose main effect is to waste trees.

Isobar Press

- isobarpress.com
- London | Founded 2013
- Editor: Paul Rossiter
- Single-Author Collections
- Submissions welcome (see website for details).

Isobar Press, founded in 2013 and based in London and Tokyo, publishes English-language poetry from Japan; rather than having any specific stylistic agenda, the press strives to represent both the variety and the excellence of the work being done there. The overall aims of the press are to ensure that the work of English-language poets associated with Japan is available, and to make Japan more visible as a location for contemporary writing. As of summer 2016, the press has published eighteen books by fourteen authors. Twelve of these writers are native-speakers of English, whether American, Canadian, English, or Irish, but two are Japanese poets who choose to write in English; in 2017 Isobar plans to begin publishing modernist and contemporary Japanese poetry in translation.

Jonathan Cape

- penguinrandomhouse.co.uk
- Founded 1921
- Editor: Robin Robertson

Part of the Penguin Random House group, the Cape poetry list includes major voices such as Alice Oswald, John Burnside and Michael Longley alongside newer voices, including Fiona Benson and Ocean Vuong.

Katabasis

- katabasis.co.uk
- London | Founded 1967
- Unsolicited submissions not currently accepted.

Katabasis has published pamphlets since 1967 and books since 1989, both poetry and prose. We publish English poetry and bilingual editions of Latin American poetry. The latter may have introductions, notes and pictures to set the poems in context. Besides publishing two of the best known Chilean poets now living in London, we are enthusiastic publishers of the poetry of Nicaragua, a country famous for its poets. From Mexico Katabasis publishes the best-selling *Zapatista Stories* by Subcomandante Marcos. Katabasis is also strongly attached to its home in London and to its native English language, landscape and radical tradition. We publish a distinctive list of English poetry and prose. We are local and internationalist, wanting down-to-Earth poetry, that is both rooted in a particular place and history, and speaks beyond them.

Kettillonia

- kettillonia.co.uk
- Angus, Scotland | Founded 1999

Kettillonia is an independent publisher based in Angus, Scotland. We aim to put into print original, adventurous, neglected and rare writing. We have a special interest in writing from Scotland or with a Scottish connection, and in work in the Scots and Gaelic languages.

Knives Forks and Spoons Press

- knivesforksandspoonspress.co.uk
- Newton-le-Willows | 2010
- Editor: Alec Newman
- Pamphlets, Single-Author Collections, Anthologies, Books about Poetry
- Submissions welcome only in specific reading windows (see website for details).

KFS publishes and promotes experimental literature.

Lapwing Publications

- freewebs.com/lapwingpoetry
- Belfast, N. Ireland | Founded 1988

Lapwing has published some of Ireland's best known authors, including James Simmons, Padraig Fiacc, Robert Greacen, Padraig O'Snodaigh, Deirdre Brennan, Michael Fanning, Des O'Grady, John Liddy, Sam Burnside, Fred Johnston, Maurice Harmon, Gerry McDonnell, and Jack Holland.

Laudanum

- laudanumpublishing.co.uk | info@laudanumpublishing.co.uk
- London | Founded 2016
- Editor: Tiffany Anne Tondut
- Anthologies, Chapbook Anthologies
- Submissions welcome only in specific reading windows (see website for details).

Laudanum is a London-based publisher of anthologies. Our themed anthologies are open to submissions, while our chapbook anthologies are commission only and feature the work of three distinctive poets per volume. Chapbooks are, on average, 10 poems in length, and yet these slim volumes afford the author extraordinary scope and flexibility, or a niche for shorter projects. Although quality is a measure of success, these anthologies aren't simply a vehicle for 'the best', but a means to disseminate verse that is exciting and inspiring for poets and public alike – a healthy mix of sex and cerebrum, philosophy and play, poetry of the moment and the considered avant-garde.

Leafe Press

- leafepress.com
- Nottingham | Founded 2000

Leafe Press was launched at a reading in Nottingham in April 2000, and has published a wide range of poetry, though our main interest at present is in innovative or experimental poetry. Poets published by Leafe Press include Catherine Wagner, Ed Baker, Tilla Brading, Adrian Buckner, Kelvin Corcoran, Peter Dent, Abdellatif Laâbi, Carrie Etter, Lee Harwood, Geraldine Monk, Martin Stannard, Simon Perril, Ernesto Priego, Peter Riley and Tristan Tzara.

Like This Press

- likethispress.wordpress.com | likethis@likethispress.co.uk
- Manchester | Founded 2012
- Editor: Nikolai Duffy
- Pamphlets, Single-Author Collections, Books about Poetry
- Unsolicited submissions not currently accepted.

Like This is a small, private press committed to publishing high quality and beautifully designed books that do things just a little bit differently. The press is particularly interested in poetry, prose poetry, fragments, creative non-fiction, interviews, essays, and books as objects.

The Literary Pocket Book

- literarypocketblog.wordpress.com
- Pontypridd | Founded 2007
- Editors: Steven Hitchins, John Maher
- Pamphlets
- Unsolicited submissions not currently accepted.

We publish experimental poetry and prose, often exploring unusual book-forms such as accordions and z-books, sometimes in miniature.

Litmus Publishing

- litmuspublishing.co.uk
- UK | Founded 2013
- Editors: Dorothy Lehane, Elinor Cleghorn
- Pamphlets, *Litmus Magazine*
- Submissions welcome (see website for details).

Litmus publishing explores the interaction between poetry and science, and is open to submissions from writers who have a full length collection or pamphlet on a scientific theme.

Little Island Press

- littleislandpress.co.uk | info@littleislandpress.co.uk

- Cotswolds | Founded 2015
- Editor: Andrew Latimer; Assistant Editor: Jessica Kelly
- Single-Author Collections, Books about Poetry
- Submissions welcome (see website for details).

Little Island Press is an independent publisher of new and classic poetry, non-fiction and international literature in translation. Based in the Cotswolds, it is the work of a few dedicated individuals who believe that great literature survives in great books: each one a little island of its own.

Liverpool University Press (Pavilion Press)

- liverpooluniversitypress.co.uk
- Liverpool

Pavilion Poetry seeks to publish the very best in contemporary poetry. Always international in reach, Pavilion Poetry is poetry that takes a risk. Whether by new or established and award-winning writers, this is poetry sure to challenge and delight.

The Littoral Press

- southendpoetry.co.uk/littoral/press.htm
- Suffolk

The Littoral Press has published poets including Maggie Freeman, Judy Gahagan and Mervyn Linford.

Longbarrow Press

- longbarrowpress.com | longbarrowpress@gmail.com
- Sheffield | Founded 2006

- Editor: Brian Lewis
- Pamphlets, Single-Author Collections, Anthologies
- Unsolicited submissions not currently accepted.

Longbarrow Press is a Sheffield-based independent poetry publisher with a reputation for work that explores the intersections of landscape, history and memory. Since the launch of our first publications in 2006, we've developed an eclectic programme of events, including poetry walks, exhibitions and collaborations with musicians and filmmakers, alongside a growing online archive of field recordings based on our visits to canals, chapels and sea caves in Yorkshire and beyond. Our parallel journey in print has also unfolded with an emphasis on innovation, with titles ranging from maps, acetates and matchboxes to our current series of acclaimed hardback books. An ethos of craft and care informs this preoccupation with 'the book as object', and helps to ensure that the format of publication is always a sympathetic response to the poem (rather than an object imposed on the poem).

Mariscat Press

- mariscatpress.com
- Edinburgh
- Editor: Hamish Whyte
- Mostly Pamphlets
- Submissions welcome (see website for details).

Mariscat is now one of the longest running self-funded small presses in Scotland, known for its tastefully designed publications and a quality backlist which includes work by figures such as Douglas Dunn, Diana Hendry and Brian McCabe, as well as numerous publications by Edwin Morgan.

Last year they won the Michael Marks Award for publishers and both the first and second prize in the Callum MacDonald Memorial Awards. They had pamphlets out recently from Jackie Kay, Stuart Conn and Tom Pow.

Materials

- material-s.blogspot.co.uk

Materials publish a magazine, *Materials*, as well as pamphlets of poetry and prose. Recent publications include works by Peter Gizzi, Kenneth Irby and Ed Luker, as well as *Brexit Borders Kill*, made quickly as a front against the fascist implications of the 'Leave' vote.

The Melos Press

- melospress.blogspot.com
- London | Founded 2007
- Editor: William Palmer
- Pamphlets, Single-Author Collections
- Unsolicited submissions not currently accepted.

Melos Press aim to publish four to six pamphlets a year of contemporary poetry by both new and established poets. The ideal pamphlet collection for us is a sequence of poems related by theme, or a single continuous narrative. We look for a high level of linguistic and poetic skill and the ability to combine lyrical and personal poetry with political and social awareness – a fairly tough combination to achieve. Our growing list includes writers such as A.C. Bevan, Jo Dixon, Cathy Galvin, David Morley, Nicholas Murray and Ian Parks. We are always on the lookout for new and promising writers.

Metre Editions

- metre-editions.com
- Editors: Justin Quinn, David Wheatley
- Chapbooks, Single-Author Collections

Metre Editions is the associated imprint of Metre, a poetry journal edited by Justin Quinn and David Wheatley between 1996 and 2005. We have published chapbooks by Evan Rail, Jane Yeh, Vona Groarke, and Harry Clifton, and recently published Cathal McCabe's *Outer Space: Selected Poems*. At present we have no immediate plans for future publications, but are open to approaches.

MIEL

- miel-books.com | miel.books@gmail.com
- Belgium | Founded 2011
- Editors: Éireann Lorsung, Andrea Beltran
- Pamphlets, Artists' Books, *1110* (magazine) (including the work of UK-based poets)
- Submissions welcome only in specific reading windows (see website for details).

MIEL was established in 2011 to promote and publish difficult, innovative, intelligent, and deeply felt writing and visual art. The press's initial focus on supporting and promoting the work of women writers has broadened, and MIEL's remit is now to publish difficult, innovative, intelligent, and deeply felt writing and artwork, with a focus on work made by women, people of color, and LGBTQ people.

Mother's Milk Books

- mothersmilkbooks.com | teika@mothersmilkbooks.com
- Nottingham | Founded 2011
- Editor: Dr Teika Bellamy
- Pamphlets, Single-Author Collections, Anthologies
- Submissions welcome only in specific reading windows (see website for details).

Mother's Milk Books is an independent press managed by at-home mother, Dr Teika Bellamy. The press was founded in 2011 with the view to publish books that normalize breastfeeding and celebrate femininity and empathy. Teika was the 2015 recipient of the Women in Publishing's 'New Venture Award' for pioneering work on behalf of under-represented groups in society; Mother's Milk Books was also longlisted in the 2016 Saboteur Awards category 'Most Innovative Publisher'.

Mudfog Press

- mudfog.press
- Teesside | Founded 1995
- Editors: Pauline Plummer, Jo Heather, Liz Geraghty, David Lynch
- Pamphlets, Single-Author Collections, Anthologies
- Submissions welcome only in specific reading windows (see website for details).

We mainly publish first time writers in the Tees Valley, defined as from Whitby to Sunderland and West to Darlington, but sometimes make an exception to this when we receive a wonderful submission. Most of our publications are beautifully designed pamphlets.

Neon Books

- neonbooks.org.uk | info@neonmagazine.co.uk
- Hampshire | Founded 2008
- Editor: Krishan Coupland
- Pamphlets, Neon Literary Magazine
- Submissions welcome (see website for details).

Neon Books curates and publishes *Neon* – an independent, UK-based literary magazine which features a selection of fiction, poetry, comics, art and illustration. *Neon* mixes literary and slipstream writing, with a particular focus on the surreal and strange. Neon Books also publishes occasional carefully-selected chapbooks, containing poetry or prose by individual authors, as well as a number of free pamphlets and a literary blog. They are based in the UK, but all of their publications are available in print and online anywhere in the world.

New Departures/Poetry Olympics

- poetryolympics.com | info@poetryolympics.com
- West London | Founded 1959
- Founder: Michael Horovitz; Editor / Publisher / Torchbearer / Curator / Producer / Presenter: Vanessa Vie; Co-Editor New Departures/Co-Producer Poetry Olympics: Adam Horovitz
- Pamphlets, Single-Author Collections, Anthologies, CDs, DVDs, Film, Vinyl Recordings, Programmes to Poetry Olympics, Jazz Poetry SuperJams & Other Events, New Departures/Poetry Olympics (magazine)

Because of continuingly hopeless finances & also declining health of Michael Horovitz, there is little scope for either publishing, or presenting as performers, more than perhaps 5-15% of contributors who have not already been involved in the 57 years of page, recorded & public stage writer/artist/performers. When New Departures & Live New Departures were founded by Michael Horovitz in his last student year as an Ox, they avowed commitment to the experimental, heterodox, internationalist, multi-medic, beat & socio-pacifist tendencies in all the arts. After the first few issues the TLS dubbed NDs "the most substantial avant-garde magazine in Gt Britain". In June 1965 LNDs co-organised The First International Poetry Incarnation which packed out London's Albert Hall & – filmed as 'Wholly Communion' – continues to inspire further innovatory developments. 'The POT! (Poetry Olympics Twenty05)' megagig & ND Anthology demonstrated how much had evolved over the 4 decades after, as again has the 'POEM! (Poetry Olympics Marathon)' 2012 event & double-DVD. Print/recorded NDs are only up to #40, but the far more frequent Jazz Poetry SuperJams & Poetry Olympics look to go on providing ever newer departures for a better future.

Nine Arches Press

- ninearchespress.com | mail@ninearchespress.com
- Midlands | Founded 2008
- Editor: Jane Commane
- Single-Author Collections, Anthologies, Books about Poetry, *Under the Radar* (magazine)
- Submissions welcome only in specific reading windows (see website for details).

At Nine Arches Press, our focus is on new adventures in poetry. We place a high value on good, concise editing and in working closely with all of our authors and poets to ensure handsome publications that we will both be proud to put our names to. Our status as an independent press gives us freedom to take risks and to closely support the writers whose work we really believe in. Nine Arches' aim as an independently-minded press is to produce books that similarly independently-minded readers will enjoy and appreciate. When looking for new writers to publish, the priority is always towards work that will excite, challenge and surprise readers. We aim also to create poetry books that readers will delight in, find thought-provoking, and return to again and again. Join us on the adventure.

Off_Press

- off-press.org

OFF_PRESS is an independent publisher promoting contemporary creative writing in English, with a special focus on translations, using multimedia and live events to celebrate reading and storytelling in different languages/genres around the world.

Offa's Press

- offaspress.co.uk
- West Midlands | Founded 2011

Offa's Press is dedicated to publishing and promoting the best in contemporary West Midland poetry and poets.

The Onslaught Press

- onslaughtpress.tumblr.com
- Oxford | Founded 2013
- Editor: Mathew D. Staunton

- Submissions welcome (see website for details).

Onslaught is particularly interested in Irish Studies, poetry, local history, children's history and picture books.

Original Plus

- thesamsmith.webs.com | smithsssj@aol.com
- Bridgend, South Wales | Founded 1996
- Editor: Sam Smith
- Pamphlets, Single-Author Collections, *The Journal* (once 'of Contemporary Anglo-Scandinavian Poetry')
- Submissions welcome (see website for details).

Our editorial policy is to try to publish those poems – from wheresoever they may come – written with thought to what the poem is saying and to how it is being said. Also welcomed are poems that can travel, that can cross boundaries, that do not assume in their readers a shared knowledge nor a shared set of beliefs. And it will be a rare day when I take a poem about being a poet or about the writing of poems. Also, because my aim is to keep *The Journal* secular, any poem containing religious terminology will not be considered for publication...

Otley Word Feast Press

- owfpress.com | books@owfpress.com
- West Yorkshire | Founded 2014
- Managing Editor: Peter White, Jane Kitsen
- Pamphlets, Single-Author Collections, Anthologies
- Unsolicited submissions not currently accepted.

Otley Word Feast Press was founded in order to produce

Spokes, an anthology of bicycle poetry to celebrate 'Le Grand Départ' of the 2014 Tour de France in Yorkshire. Following this success, it was decided to produce pamphlets and collections to showcase the works of poets who write and engage in the various literary activities in and around the town of Otley. Anthologies of nation-wide poetry have also been produced on the themes of 'The Garden', 'Otley' and 'Pubs'.

Oversteps Books Ltd

- overstepsbooks.com | alwynmarriage@overstepsbooks.com
- Devon | Founded 1992
- Managing Editor: Alwyn Marriage
- Single-Author Collections
- Submissions welcome (see website for details).

We seek to publish the best in contemporary poetry, with our poets chosen blind by an Editorial Board. Not only the standard of the poetry, but also the quality of the finished books is exceptionally high.

Oystercatcher Press

- oystercatcherpress.com
- Norfolk | Founded 2007
- Editor: Peter Hughes
- Pamphlets
- Unsolicited submissions not currently accepted.

Oystercatcher has published a very wide range of contemporary poetry. It is particularly interested in performance writing for the page.

Paekakariki Press

- paekakarikipress.com | matt@paekakarikipress.com
- London | Founded 2010
- Editor: Matt McKenzie
- Single-Author Collections, Anthologies
- Submissions welcome (see website for details).

We aim to publish new work from previously unpublished poets and to encourage collaborations between poets and artists. The books are printed on letterpress machinery salvaged from the scrap heap.

Paper Swans Press

- paperswans.co.uk
- Kent/Sussex | Founded 2014
- Editors: Sarah Miles, Ellie Danak
- Pamphlets, Single-Author Collections, Anthologies
- Submissions welcome only in specific reading windows (see website for details).

Paper Swans is a small, independent press, passionate about publishing poetry and flash fiction. They are especially keen to provide a platform for emerging writers, but also have some wonderful, established poets published in their anthologies. This year, they published their first single-author pamphlets: Elisabeth Sennitt Clough's *Glass* and Lydia Popowich's *The Jellyfish Society*. Currently, they are seeking submissions for a Young Adult anthology, asking for poets aged 13-18 to submit and hoping to give a platform to younger voices in poetry. Although based in the UK, they welcome submissions from writers all over the world. Last year, they co-founded 'The

Poetry Shelf' with Abegail Morley and Jill Munro, with a mission to bring more poetry to their local communities in Kent/Sussex. Paper Swans most recent event was at The National Trust's Sissinghurst Castle, where winners from their 'Roses' competition read in the gardens of Vita Sackville-West.

Parthian Books

- parthianbooks.com
- Cardigan, West Wales | Founded 1993

The company was established in 1993 by Publishing Director Richard Lewis Davies to publish his first novel, *Work, Sex and Rugby*. Parthian has risen to become one of the most respected publishers in Wales – and one with international resonance and an innovative range of new fiction, poetry and drama.

Partus Press

- partuspress.com | partus@partuspress.com
- Manchester | Founded 2012
- Director: Valgerður Thorodds
- Pamphlets, Single-Author Collections, Anthologies
- Submissions welcome (see website for details).

Partus is an independent publisher committed to the discovery of contemporary Icelandic and international literature. Founded in Reykjavík, Iceland, the press is now based between the Icelandic capital and Manchester, England – publishing emerging Icelandic authors, as well as poetry in translation, and contemporary UK poets.

Peepal Tree Press

- peepaltreepress.com | contact@peepaltreepress.com
- Leeds | Founded 1985
- Managing Editor: Jeremy Poynting; Associate Poetry Editor: Kwame Dawes
- Single-Author Collections, Anthologies, Books about Poetry
- Submissions welcome (see website for details).

Peepal Tree Press is the leading publisher of Caribbean and Black British fiction and poetry. We publish on average twenty titles a year and have around 350 titles in print, of which around a third are poetry titles. Poets we have published include: Lauren Alleyne, Edward Baugh, Kamau Brathwaite, Malika Booker, Christian Campbell, Vahni Capildeo, Merle Collins, Mahadai Das, Kwame Dawes, Kendel Hippolyte, Ishion Hutchinson, Anthony Kellman, Loretta Collins Klobah, Vladimir Lucien, Shara McCallum, Mark McWatt, Nii Parkes, Jennifer Rahim, Eric Roach, Roger Robinson, Tanya Shirley and many others.

Penguin Books

- penguinrandomhouse.co.uk
- Editor: Donald Futers

Part of the Penguin Random House group, the recently invigorated Penguin list includes work by Anne Carson, Emily Berry and Sophie Collins.

Penned in the Margins

- pennedinthemargins.co.uk |

info@pennedinthemargins.co.uk

- London| Founded 2004
- Editor: Tom Chivers
- Single-Author Collections, Anthologies, Books about Poetry, Literary Fiction, Creative Non-Fiction, Novellas
- Submissions welcome (see website for details).

Penned in the Margins creates publications and performances for people who are not afraid to take risks. They believe in the power of language to challenge how we think, test new ideas and explore alternative stories, publishing poetry, creative non-fiction, literary fiction and criticism that seeks to do the same. From small beginnings as a reading series in a converted railway arch in south London, Penned in the Margins has grown over the last decade to be a respected literary arts company producing new work live, in print and online. This unique blend of publishing and production characterises their distinctive model in the cultural landscape; in 2015 they joined Arts Council England's National Portfolio.

Picador

- picador.com
- London | Founded 1972
- Editor: Don Paterson
- Single-Author Collections, Anthologies, Books about Poetry
- Unsolicited submissions not currently accepted.

What defines a Picador book is the author's voice: Picador believes the way the story is told is just as important as the story itself, and this is the case for fiction, non-fiction and poetry. Picador publishes writers from all over the world, bringing international authors to an English-language readership and providing a platform for voices that are often not heard. We publish a list that includes literary fiction; new, relevant and challenging fiction; narrative non-fiction; authoritative, cultural non-fiction; and the best contemporary poetry; as well as a number of uncategorizable books that will surprise you. We also aim to make beautiful books, from exciting and original first publications to clean, elegantly designed commercial paperbacks.

Pindrop Press

- pindroppress.com | editor@pindroppress.com
- UK & France | Founded 2010
- Editor: Sharon Black
- Single-Author Collections
- Submissions welcome (see website for details).

Pindrop Press is a small, independent poetry publisher based in France with its headquarters in Glasgow. Its mission is to publish poetry that is exciting, juicy and innovative.

Platypus Press

- platypuspress.co.uk | enquiries@platypuspress.co.uk
- Shropshire | Founded 2015
- Editor: Michelle Tudor; Creative Director: Peter Barnfather
- Pamphlets, Single-Author Collections, Anthologies, Digital Chapbooks, *Wildness* (magazine - readwildness.com)
- Submissions welcome (see website for details).

Platypus Press is an independent publisher based in England that seeks to unearth innovative contemporary poetry and prose from a broad variety of voices and experiences.

Poem Flyer

- facebook.com/PoemFlyer
- Leicestershire | Founded 2015
- Editor: Robert Richardson
- Single Poem Flyers
- Unsolicited submissions not currently accepted.

Poem Flyer brings together a design and print format with a corresponding editorial focus. This is a conscious affiliation with the Imagist principles of conciseness of form and precision of language. The older foundations of lyric and epigram are also, inevitably, present. As typography, it is an entertaining imprint, but the content of some of the poems present a serious side.

Poetry Saltzburg

- poetrysalzburg.com
- Austria | Founded 1998
- Submissions welcome (see website for details).
- Pamphlets, Single-Author Collections, *Poetry Salzburg Review* (including the work of UK-based poets)

Publisher of a regular journal, pamphlets and books. Recent publications include works by Vuyelwa Carlin, Jane Bonnyman and Scott Elder.

Poetry Space Ltd

- poetryspace.co.uk | susan@poetryspace.co.uk
- Bristol | Founded 2010
- Editor: Susan Sims

- Pamphlets, Single-Author Collections, Anthologies, Online Poetry Showcase

We are reading submissions for the online showcase of poetry published quarterly but not reading submissions for collections at the moment. Poetry Space Ltd is non profit making organisation and their mission is to widen participation in poetry through online challenges, competitions, workshops and the online Poetry Space Showcase Quarterly and to bring more poets to recognition through pamphlet and book publication. The Photo and Poem challenge which has recently closed has gathered many avid followers and the resulting photographs and poems will be published in a book. They operate a membership scheme for readers who want to help support Poetry Space activities, with members receiving a quarterly package of publications including a printed edition of the online showcase and a surprise publication drawn from their growing collection of books and pamphlets. They have also helped several poets raise money for specific causes through pamphlet publication.

Polygon (an imprint of Birlinn Ltd)

- polygonbooks.co.uk | poetry@polygonbooks.co.uk
- Edinburgh | Founded 1992
- Poetry Editor: Edward Crossan
- Single-Author Collections, Anthologies, Books about Poetry
- Submissions welcome (see website for details).

Polygon was originally set up by students of the University of Edinburgh and publishes literary fiction – both classic and modern – from Scottish writers such as Robin Jenkins, George Mackay Brown and Kevin MacNeil; and poetry including Norman MacCaig, Sorley MacLean and Liz Lochhead.

PYRAMID Editions

- pyramideditions.co.uk | owen@pyramideditions.co.uk
- London | 2015
- Managing Editor: Owen Vince
- Pamphlets
- Submissions welcome only in specific reading windows (see website for details).

PYRAMID Editions publishes the work of writers aged 30 and under. It emphasizes a poetry of formal experimentation, cross-disciplinarity, and linguistic 'estrangement'. Each 'shortbook' features three poems by one author, focused on a specific concept, image, or event; a proximity of encounter and visualization.

Rack Press

- rackpress.blogspot.com | rackpress@nicholasmurray.co.uk
- Powys, Wales | Founded 2005
- Publisher: Nicholas Murray
- Pamphlets, Books About Poetry
- Submissions welcome (see website for details).

Rack Press has a very open editorial policy and welcomes all kinds of poetry provided that, if we are lucky, it is well-crafted, intelligent, coherent and richly imagined. Cliques, coteries and people-like-us are not our bag.

Ragged Lion Press

- raggedlionpress.co.uk
- Submissions welcome (see website for details).

Ragged Lion Press are a publisher of literature and art, with a focus on traditional methods of print. They have recently published work by Jeremy Reed and Charles Plymell.

Reality Street

- realitystreet.co.uk | ken@realitystreet.co.uk
- Hastings | 1993
- Editor: Ken Edwards
- Single-Author Collections, Anthologies
- Unsolicited submissions not currently accepted.

Between 1993 and 2016 Reality Street published new and innovative poetry and prose from Britain and elsewhere. Extensive backlist available.

Red Ceilings

- theredceilingspress.co.uk

Red Ceilings publish poetry in their ebook series, chapbooks and on their blog, and like innovative, experimental and avant-garde work in particular.

Red Squirrel Press

- redsquirrelpress.com | editor@redsquirrelpress.com
- Northumberland | Founded 2006
- Editor: Sheila Wakefield
- Pamphlets, Single-Author Collections
- Submissions welcome (see website for details)

Red Squirrel Press is an independent publisher based in

Northumberland, founded by Editor Sheila Wakefield. It publishes mainly poetry – pamphlets and single-author collections – but also crime fiction novels, short story pamphlets and collections, novellas and non-fiction. Red Squirrel Press has published over 160 titles to date and publishes established poets such as William Bedford and Pippa Little as well as new talent such as Andrew McMillan and Claire Askew.

The Rialto

- therialto.co.uk | info@therialto.co.uk
- Norwich | 1984
- Editor: Michael Mackmin; Assistant Editors: Rishi Dastidar, Edward Doegar, Holly Hopkins, Fiona Moore, Abigail Parry, Degna Stone
- *The Rialto* (magazine), Pamphlets, occasional Single-Author Collections
- Magazine submissions are welcome (see website for details).

The magazine's founding editors, Michael among them, believed in a 'Republic of Poetry', an inclusive and diverse world of poetry open to experiment in form and content. The current team strive to keep this vision alive. *The Rialto* magazine appears three times a year and each issue, with its spacious A4 pages, has fifty or so poems, an editorial and occasional, commissioned, prose pieces. Most space is occupied by the best new poems the editors can find, wrapped in famously vibrant covers. *The Rialto* publishes pamphlets in its Bridge series (Laura Scott's *What I Saw* won the Michael Marks Award in 2014) and occasionally a full collection. This year sees the first ever pamphlet competition, judged by *Rialto* poet Hannah Lowe, deadline end November. Since 2013 *The Rialto* has run an Editor Development Programme, supported by the Arts Council, to bring new people to editing and new perspectives to the magazine.

Rockingham Press

- rockingham1.webspace.virginmedia.com
- Ware, Herts | Founded 1991

Rockingham Press was set up to champion new and neglected poets and also Middle East poetry in translation. Since then Rockingham has published each year on average four paperback collections (always including a first collection) and one or two pamphlets. Its Middle East titles have included *Modern Turkish Poetry* (a PBS recommendation), *Modern Persian Poetry*, and works by Feyyaz Kayacan Fergar and Oktay Rifat.

Roncadora Press

- hughbryden.com | roncadorapress@gmail.com
- Dumfries | Founded 2005
- Editor: Hugh Bryden
- Pamphlets, Artists' Books
- Unsolicited submissions not currently accepted.

Roncadora Press wishes to place itself where artists books and poetry pamphlets comfortably meet, to have the handmade and individual feel of an artists book combined with quality contemporary poetry. The marriage of word and image is the main concern.

Route

- route-online.com

Route was founded in 2000 and has an eclectic author list.

Sad Press

- sadpress.wordpress.com | sophiestamina@gmail.com
- Bristol | Founded 2010
- Editors: Jo & Samantha Walton
- Pamphlets, *Hix Eros* (magazine)
- Open to submissions from Mallory Ortberg, Elif Batuman, Steve Aylett, Tim Morris, M. John Harrison, Caitlín Doherty, Anne Laure Coxam, Eley Williams, Yoon Ha Lee, Connie Scozzaro, Sofia Samatar, Holly Pester, Sophie Robinson, and Lila Matsumoto.

Sad Press focuses on experimental and political writing. Together with Hi Zero (Ed. Joe Luna) it publishes *Hix Eros: Poetry Review*, which features criticism, reviews, and responses to contemporary poetry.

Salò Press

- salopress.weebly.com | editorsalopress@gmail.com
- Norwich | Founded 2015
- Editor: Sophie Essex
- Single-Author Collections, Anthologies, *Fur-Lined Ghettos* (magazine)
- Submissions welcome (see website for details).

Salò Press is an orgiastic love affair.

Salt Publishing

- saltpublishing.com
- Norfolk | Founded 1999
- Unsolicited submissions not currently accepted.

Currently publishes an annual *Best British Poetry* anthology. Some single-author collections from its substantial backlist remain available via their website.

Seren

- serenbooks.com | amylwack@aol.com
- Bridgend, Wales | Founded 1980
- Poetry Editor: Amy Wack; Managing Editor: Mick Felton
- Pamphlets, Single-Author Collections, Anthologies, *Poetry Wales* (magazine)
- Submissions welcome (see website for details).

Seren publish poetry in English and often feature writers from Wales. We have established a reputation for quality. We like intelligence, formal skill, flair.

Shearsman Books

- shearsman.com | editor@shearsman.com
- Bristol | Founded 1981
- Editor: Tony Frazer
- Pamphlets, Single-Author Collections, Anthologies, Books about Poetry, *Shearsman* (magazine)
- Reading windows for the magazine. Open submissions for the press.

In terms of Shearsman's position with regard to contemporary poetry, there is a clear inclination towards the more exploratory end of the current spectrum. Notwithstanding this, however, quality work of a more conservative kind will always be considered seriously, provided that the work is well-written. (Thus, we published a fine volume of formal verse by Erica McAlpine in 2016, but two months later published a volume of entirely visual poetry from Irish poet, Susan Connolly.) What I do not like at all is sloppy writing of any kind; I always look for some rigour in the work, although we will be more forgiving of failure in this regard if the writer is trying to push out the boundaries. I tend to like mixing work from both ends of the spectrum in the magazine, and firmly believe that good writing can, and should, cohabit with other forms of good writing, regardless of the aesthetic that drives it, and regardless of whether the practitioners are happy about such cohabitation.

Shit Valley

- shitvalley.tumblr.com | shitvalleyverlag@gmail.com

SHIT VALLEY PUBLISHES LABORIOUSLY CHEAP PAMPHLETS BY MORALLY EXPENSIVE POETS, AT A BIAS OUT OF CAMBRIDGE UK. WE ACCEPT CASH, CHEQUES, OR FOOD OF ANY TYPE.

Shoestring Press

- shoestringpress.co.uk | info@shoestringpress.co.uk
- Nottinghamshire | Founded 1994
- Editor: John Lucas
- Pamphlets, Single-Author Collections, Books about Poetry
- Unsolicited submissions not currently accepted.

We specialise in publishing poetry sequences and collections, usually by established but unfashionable poets and poets we are introducing to British readers for the first time, though they may be well known elsewhere.

Sidekick Books

- sidekickbooks.com
- London | Founded 2009
- Editors: Kirsten Irving, Jon Stone
- Anthologies, Collaborative Projects
- Unsolicited submissions not currently accepted.

Sidekick Books is the improbable imprint of disgraced alchemist Dr Fulminare, and its publications are the produce of his infernal book lab, in which volatile fusions are mixed with reckless abandon: poetry, comics, film, video games, dinosaurs, astrophysics, and more. Sidekick's specialisms are collaborative works, multi-poet anthologies/treasuries, and experimental medium-mixing. They also do a strong line in books engaging with the natural world and its relationship to humans.

Silhouette Press

- silhouettepress.co.uk | adam.steiner@silhouettepress.co.uk
- Coventry | Founded 2013
- Editors: Adam Steiner, Raef Boylan, Matt Barton
- Poetry, *Here Comes Everone* (magazine)
- Submissions welcome (see website for details).

Silhouette Press is a not-for-profit social enterprise publisher that aims to improve access to the publishing industry. We are open to submissions of poetry, fiction and non-fiction. We also publish *Here Comes Everyone*, a bi-monthly literary magazine of fiction, articles and poetry (you can read it at: www.herecomeseveryone.me).

SINE WAVE PEAK

- sinewavepeak.com | luke@sinewavepeak.com
- Manchester | Founded 2012
- Director: Luke Allan; Managing Editor: Valgerdur Thorodds
- Pamphlets, Single-Author Collections, Anthologies, Fugitive Editions, Poem Cards, Object Poems
- Submissions welcome (see website for details).

SINE WAVE PEAK is a small press that specializes in contemporary concrete and formal poetry. Recent editions include work by Thomas A Clark, Aram Saroyan, Hannah Lowe, Jerome Rothenberg, and Pam Rehm. Upcoming editions include work by Tom Betteridge, Mary Ellen Solt, and Robin Boothroyd.

Singing Apple Press

- singingapplepress.com | info@singingapplepress.com
- Somerset | Founded 2014
- Editor: Camilla Nelson
- Limited Edition Artist Books and Poetry Objects
- Unsolicited submissions not currently accepted.

Founded in 2014, Singing Apple Press is devoted to the material investigation of poem production, particularly in relation to plants. This small, Somerset-based press produces hand-crafted, limited edition poem-prints, books and other poem objects.

smith|doorstop Books

- poetrybusiness.co.uk | office@poetrybusiness.co.uk
- Sheffield | Founded 1986
- Editors: Peter & Ann Sansom
- Pamphlets, Single-Author Collections, Anthologies, *The North* (magazine)
- Submissions welcome only in specific reading windows (see website for details).

The Poetry Business has lasted for 30 years on the mainstay of all the independent presses: enthusiasm. They are committed to finding and nurturing the work of new poets and do this through their annual Book and Pamphlet Competition, New Poets' Prize for poets aged 16-22 and the Laureate's Choice series of pamphlets selected by Carol Ann Duffy. Many of their more established poets have been discovered through these channels and gone on to produce several poetry collections with the press.

Smokestack Books

- smokestack-books.co.uk | info@smokestack-books.co.uk
- North Yorkshire | Founded 2004
- Editor: Andy Croft
- Single-Author Collections, Anthologies
- Submissions welcome (see website for details).

Smokestack aims to keep open a space for what is left of the English radical poetic tradition in the twenty-first century. Smokestack champions poets who are unfashionable, radical, left-field and working a long way from the metropolitan centres of cultural authority. Smokestack is interested in the World as well as the Word; believes that poetry is a part of and not apart from society; argues that if poetry does not belong to everyone it is not poetry. Smokestack's list includes books by John Berger, Katrina Porteous, Ian McMillan, Kate Fox, Martin Rowson, Tom Leonard, Sebastian Barker, Gerda Stevenson and Steve Ely. Smokestack's growing international list includes books by Bertolt Brecht (Germany), Roque Dalton (El Salvador), Gustavo Pereira (Venezuela), Rocco Scotellaro (Italy), Heinrich Heine (Germany), Nicola Vaptsarov (Bulgaria), Francis Combes (France), Andras Mezei (Hungary), Yiannis Ritsos (Greece) and Victor Jara (Chile).

Soundswrite Press

- soundswritepress.co.uk | soundswrite@ntlworld.com
- Leicester | Founded 2005
- Co-ordinator: Karin Koller (co-ordinator); Editors: Marilyn Ricci and DA Prince
- Pamphlets, Single-Author Collections, Anthologies
- Unsolicited submissions not currently accepted.

Soundswrite Press publishes pamphlets, single-author collections and anthologies of poetry by women attending Soundswrite, an open group based in the East Midlands. The latest anthology includes poems by 17 women.

Stairwell Books

- stairwellbooks.co.uk | dreamcatchermagazine.co.uk | rose@stairwellbooks.com
- Yorkshire | Founded 2005
- Proprietors: Rose Drew & Alan Gillott; *Dream Catcher* Editor: John Gilham
- Single-Author Collections, Anthologies, Memoirs, Verse

Plays, *Dream Catcher* (magazine)
- Submissions welcome (see website for details).

Stairwell Books looks for good writing in any genre. Though a link with York or Yorkshire helps, we are committed to publishing good writing with a wide appeal. *Dream Catcher* is an international arts journal that accepts poetry and short prose. *Dream Catcher*'s ethos is to be eclectic and appeal to a wide readership.

Starborn Books

- starbornbooks.co.uk

Starborn has published various poets including Alex Barr, Peter Naumann and Peter Oram. Please visit their website for details.

Stinky Bear Press

- stinkybearpress.wordpress.com
- London & Liverpool | Founded 2012
- Editors: Sarah Crewe, Pascal O'Loughlin, Linus Slug.

They publish poetry zines and hold events. Zines include *Inside my head my dog's a bear* inspired by Sonic Youth, *POEM ART THREAT!* inspired by the The Fall, and *Venus as a bear* inspired by Björk. Their most recent publication *RWF/RAF* includes texts inspired by Rainer Werner Fassbinder and Ulrike Meinhof.

Stonewood Press

- stonewoodpress.co.uk
- East Northamptonshire | Founded 2011

- Editor: Martin Parker
- Pamphlets, Single-Author Collections, Anthologies, Short Fiction, Poetry Trading Cards
- Submissions welcome (see website for details).

Stonewood Press is an independent publisher dedicated to promoting new writing with an emphasis on contemporary short stories and poetry. It aims to publish challenging and high-quality writing in English without the pressures associated with mainstream publishing. Stonewood's books are beautifully designed and produced, from artists books to the Thumbprint chapbooks (as unique in the writing as the authors' fingerprints). Owner Martin Parker says: "I'm excited by the future of publishing and what book publishing could become – not only books but maybe an anthology made of up cards from the new Traverse poetry trading cards project; a series of podcasts or vlogs with no paper or ebook equivalent - the possibilities are only limited by our's and our authors' imaginations. And luckily, we have a wellspring of imagination!"

Stranger Press

- strangerpress.com | strangerpress@gmail.com
- Leeds | Founded 2013
- Editor: Chris Stephenson
- Single-Author Collections, Broadsides, chapbooks, objects
- Unsolicited submissions not currently accepted.

Stranger Press aims to be open to as wide a range of forms and ideas as possible and present contemporary, experimental and innovative writing and artwork that isn't afraid to take imaginative and linguistic risks. Our eclectic books, lo-fi chapbooks and broadsides often contain handmade elements and celebrate the weird, wonderful and the often not quite all there.

Sylph Editions

- sylpheditions.com
- London | Founded 2008

Sylph Editions publish fiction, monographs, theoretical essays, limited-edition art and photography books, and different forms of experimental writing. Most recently they brought out Anne Carson's *Nay Rather*.

the tall-lighthouse

- tall-lighthouse.co.uk
- London | Founded 1999

The tall-lighthouse publishes full collections, pamphlets, chapbooks and anthologies of poetry. They are on hiatus until 2017. Existing titles remain available for order in the meantime.

Tangerine Press

- eatmytangerine.com
- London | Founded 2006

Since 2006, Tangerine Press has pubished new, neglected and innovative writing in handbound limited editions, in tandem with more readily available paperbacks. The press's primary output is poetry and prose, with occasional photobook and spoken word releases. Tangerine has published work by James

Kelman, Billy Childish, Jack London and William Wantling, amongst many others.

Tapsalteerie

- tapsalteerie.co.uk
- Aberdeen | Founded 2013
- Editor: Duncan Lockerbie
- Submissions welcome (see website for details).

Tapsalteerie is a Scottish poetry pamphlet publisher based in rural Aberdeenshire. They produce quality poetry pamphlets written in Scots, Gaelic and English, with a focus on new poets and innovative writing.

Telltale Press

- telltalepress.co.uk | publish@telltalepress.co.uk
- Sussex | Founded 2014
- Editor: Robin Houghton
- Pamphlets
- Unsolicited submissions not currently accepted.

Telltale Press is a collective of poets. We publish primarily short, first poetry pamphlets and help develop and support one another to move forward with our poetry careers. We believe in proactivity and a spirit of co-operation and self-help, rather than competition. We bring different skills to the table – design, publishing, marketing, writing, business acumen and more. We also have an experienced poet – Catherine Smith – helping us as Associate Editor. Our pamphlets are designed to be 'calling cards' – small promotional vehicles, if you like, for a poet's work; a springboard for bigger things. We work on the basis of shared responsibility which we feel is fair, sustainable and emotionally satisfying.

Templar Poetry

- templarpoetry.com | info@templarpoetry.com
- Derbyshire | Founded 2005
- Editor: Alexander McMillen
- Pamphlets, Single-Author Collections, Anthologies, Fiction, *iOTA* (magazine)
- Submissions welcome (see website for details).

Templar Poetry is a leading, innovative independent publisher founded in 2005 and based in Derbyshire publishing excellent poets from across the British Isles. A unique annual publishing event – The Derwent Poetry Festival in Derbyshire – launched many new titles and regular Templar Poetry Live readings take place at Keats House and numerous other live readings and festivals. Submissions are welcome from new and established poets through three pamphlet awards and the annual Starid Collection Award. *iOTA* magazine publishes new poetry alongside reviews, features and fiction. Templar is committed to spoken word poetry and presents many poets on an online audio archive.

Test Centre

- testcentre.org.uk
- London | Founded 2011
- Editors: Jess Chandler & Will Shutes
- Pamphlets, Single-Author Collections, Anthologies, *Test Centre* (magazine)
- Submissions welcome only in specific reading windows (see website for details).

Test Centre is an independent publishing house and record label with an interest in the spoken and written word. We publish works by new and established writers, with a focus on experimental approaches, and a commitment to producing books and records that are beautifully designed and printed. We hope to offer to writers artistic freedom and a close engagement with the publishing process. Recent publications include work by Erik Stinson, Jen Calleja and Stephen Watts.

Thamesis Publications

- thamesispublications.co.uk
- London

A new poetry and literature publisher who has published titles by Derrick Porter and Fawzia Kane.

Tipped Press

- tippedpress.com/
- Founded 2014

Currently publishing work by David Grundy, Tomas Weber, Marianne Morris and William Ding. See website for details.

Tuba Press

- tubapress.eu | tuba poetry@icloud.com
- Gloucestershire | 1976
- Editor: Charles Graham; Assistant Editor: Peter Ellson
- Single-Author Collections
- Submissions welcome (see website for details).

We do not encourage or exclude any particular form of poetry; but we do look for work which contributes something lasting, to English Literature.

Two Rivers Press Ltd

- tworiverspress.com | tworiverspress@gmail.com
- Reading | Founded 1994
- Managing Publisher: Sally Mortimore; Poetry Editor: Peter Robinson
- Single-Author Collections, Anthologies, Classic poems, Illustrated Books
- Submissions welcome (see website for details, though a limited opportunity to accept unsolicited submissions).

Two decades of publishing and over 100 titles since its inception, Two Rivers Press has been described as 'one of the most characterful small presses in the country'. Based in Reading, its books explore and celebrate its place in the world, with local history titles as well as poetry. Bold illustration and striking design feature strongly and its contribution to Reading's culture won a Pride of Reading award in 2008.

V. Press

- vpresspoetry.blogspot.co.uk | vpresspoetry@hotmail.com
- Worcestershire | Founded 2013
- Editor: SA Leavesley
- Pamphlets, Single-Author Collections, Flash Fiction Pamphlets
- Submissions welcome only in specific reading windows (see website for details).

Established with a launch at Ledbury Poetry Festival 2013, V. Press publishes poetry and flash fiction that is very very. Our editors have eclectic tastes, with emphasis on quality over any particular style. V. Press poetry knows what it wants to do and does it well. Our rapidly expanding range of publications include Jacqui Rowe's poetry pamphlet *Ransom Notes*, Carrie Etter's flash fiction pamphlet *Hometown*, Kathy Gee's poetry collection *Book of Bones*, David Calcutt's illustrated poetry sequence *The Old Man in the House of Bone* and Claire Walker's poetry pamphlet *The Girl Who Grew Into a Crocodile*, which was chosen as one of the Poetry Book Society's 'Other New Pamphlets' for spring 2016. We currently release 4-8 titles a year and are proud to publish debut pamphlets and collections, as well as established voices.

Vagabond Voices

- vagabondvoices.co.uk
- Glasgow | Founded 2008

Vagabond Voices is committed to introducing new titles from Scottish authors and translating fiction from other languages.

Valley Press

- valleypressuk.com
- Scarborough | Founded 2008
- Editor: Jamie McGarry; Associate Editor: Rosa Campbell
- Pamphlets, Single-Author Collections, Anthologies, Fiction, Non-Fiction
- Submissions welcome only in specific reading windows (see website for details).

Valley Press books are never cynical or hateful, and aim for accessibility and literary quality at the same time – when we get it right, that's a magical combination. We do not compromise on production quality; to own a Valley Press book is to love it (if we say so ourselves). Though still a tiny organisation, we hope to play a big part in the future of poetry publishing. If you'd like to be part of that, visit our website and sign up to the newsletter – it never descends to the level of 'spam', we like to think it's more like a letter from a friend. Give it a try!

Vane Women Press

- vanewomen.co.uk
- Darlington | Founded 1993
- Editor: Jackie Litherland; Assistant Editor: Marilyn Longstaff; Art Editor: Pat Maycroft
- Pamphlets, Single-Author Collections, Anthologies
- Submissions welcome from women resident in the NE

Vane Women Press is feminist in ethos because it aims to support women writers with first pamphlet collections (poetry/short stories) as the first step in their writing career. We provide mentoring and editorial guidance if required. Vane Women is a writing, performing and publishing collective which has charitable status. It supports the Press by raising funds through readings, workshops and sales. The collective was founded in 1991 with 12 members. We aim to maintain a constant level of numbers although the membership has changed over the years. We have published anthologies and in exceptional circumstances single full collections. Our writers must have residence in the North East of England. This year we published *NORTHbound*, a mixed media anthology of photographs by Pat

Maycroft and writing by Vane Women and North East guest writers to celebrate our 25th anniversary.

Vanguard Editions

- richardskinner.weebly.com/vanguard-editions.html
- London | Founded 2014
- Editor: Richard Skinner
- Single-Author Collections, Anthologies
- Unsolicited submissions not currently accepted.

Vanguard Readings, founded in 2011, and its publishing arm Vanguard Editions, founded in 2014, were set up to promote the work of new and established authors in print and performance.

Veer Books

- veerbooks.com | veerbooks@gmail.com
- London | Founded 2003
- Veer is a collective: Adrian Clarke, Ulli Freer, Aodan McCardle, Stephen Mooney, William Rowe, Carol Watts
- Pamphlets, Single-Author Collections
- Submissions welcome (see website for details).

Veer aims to publish a range of unconforming writing in poetry and poetics, including some texts that other publishers might view as experimental. Operating between Birkbeck College and the University of Surrey, Veer Books have been encouraging new work in poetry and poetics since 2003. We have been seeking to create an audience for the now nearly 100 titles we have published through conferences, workshops and readings in a variety of contexts and locations. We remain open to work that challenges without preconceptions.

Walden Press

- waldenpress.co.uk | spike495@hotmail.com
- London | Founded 2014
- Artist / Printmaker / Publisher: Spike Gascoigne
- Pamphlets, Illustrated poetry books
- Submissions welcome (see website for details).

Walden Press specialises in small runs of letterpressed books, prints and posters. Books are hand-sewn, type is set by hand and illustrations are printed from original hand-cut woodblocks. Publications range from those of a satirical nature, often laced with a dry wit and darkly humerous illustrations, to illustrated philosophical and cultural texts and concepts. The hand-made nature of the work, being slower and more personal than the digitally printed alternative is a central theme of Walden Press publications.

Ward Wood Publishing

- wardwoodpublishing.co.uk | adele@wardwoodpublishing.co.uk
- London | Founded 2010
- Pamphlets, Single-Author Collections, Anthologies
- Unsolicited submissions not currently accepted.

Ward Wood Publishing specialises in both poetry and fiction, with an equal number of books in each form produced each year. We also publish the Bedford Square series of anthologies, featuring the work of students on the MA in Creative Writing at Royal Holloway, University of London. Authors on our list enjoy the care that goes into the edit and being involved in all stages of the cover design and book production process. We commit to our authors and they stay with us, forming a close bond and a family feel. Our authors have been selected for their originality and the exceptional quality of their writing.

Waywiser

- waywiser-press.com
- Founded 2001
- Editor-in-Chief: Philip Hoy

The Waywiser Press is a literary press, first and foremost, with a special interest in modern poetry and fiction. They are keen to promote the work of new as well as established authors.

William Cornelius Harris Publishing

- londonpoetrybooks.com | whyjason206@gmail.com
- London | Founded 2012
- Editors: Jason Why, L Harris
- Anthologies, Books about Poetry, Adventure
- Submissions welcome (see website for details).

Our goal is to help unpublished authors who have suffered from discrimination and distress to be published by providing all the tools necessary to achieve their goal.

Worple Press

- worplepress.co.uk | theworpleco@aol.com
- Tonbridge, Kent | Founded 1997
- Co-Directors: Peter & Amanda Carpenter; Publishing Assistant: Michael McKimm
- Pamphlets, Single-Author Collections, Anthologies,

Books about Poetry
- Submissions welcome only in specific reading windows (see website for details).

Worple Press publishes collections, pamphlets, anthologies, works in translation, essays, and interviews by new and established poets. We have an established reputation for high quality publication standards: books that are a pleasure to handle as well as to read. Recent authors include John Freeman, Carolyn Oulton, Linda Saunders, William Wootten, Andy Brown, Martyn Crucefix, Ben Smith and Izzy Galleymore. Small Press, Major Players.

Wrecking Ball Press

- wreckingballpress.com
- Hull | Founded 1997

Wrecking Ball Press publishes high quality, cutting edge literature, building a national reputation that far exceeds its size. Wrecking Ball Press has a strong record of discovering exciting first time writers, many of whom have gone on to have further commercial and critical success with larger publishers.

Yew Tree Press

- [not currently online] | yewtreepress@freewebs.com
- Cheltenham | Founded 1997
- Editor: Colin Honnor
- Pamphlets, Single-Author Collections, Anthologies, Books about Poetry, Editions of Artists' Work, Fine Art, Ephemera
- Submissions welcome (email for details).

The Yew Tree Press was founded to print nooks sheets, texts and graphic work by hand using the techniques of the great presses, Aldus, Estienne and The Latin Press of Guido Morris dedicated to human rights and the arts of peace. We mainly print poetry and short prose and concentrate on letterpress.

zimZalla

- zimzalla.co.uk | mail@zimzalla.co.uk
- Manchester | Founded 2009
- Editor: Tom Jenks
- Literary Objects
- Submissions welcome (see website for details).

zimZalla publishes poetry objects, with recent releases including badges, poems in styrofoam with free chips and sauce and a pair of poetic garters. zimZalla is always interested in new ideas and new forms.

Poetry Organisations

Assorted Translations

- timothyades.com | timothyades@aol.com
- London | Founded 2014

Timothy Adès manages a bookstall which selects and sells books of translated poetry, promoting poetry translation by displaying a range of books for sale at fairs and festivals.

Forward Arts Foundation

- forwardartsfoundation.org | nationalpoetryday.co.uk | info@forwardartsfoundation.org
- London | Founded 1991
- Exec. Director: Susannah Herbert; Forward Prizes Manager: Holly Hopkins
- Anthologies of poems shortlisted for the Forward Prizes

The Forward Arts Foundation is a charity committed to widening poetry's audience, honouring achievement and supporting talent, through the Forward Prizes for Poetry and the Forward Book of Poetry, an indispensable annual anthology of the year's best poetry. The Forward Prizes are awarded at a public ceremony with readings from the shortlisted poets. The 2016 Forward Prizes ceremony will be held at Southbank Centre, London, on 20 September and will be accompanied by a special anniversary anthology: *100 Prizes Poems: Twenty-five yeas of the Forward Books*. We also co-ordinate National Poetry Day, the annual mass celebration of poetry and all things poetical, which will take place on Thursday 6 October 2016 and Thursday 28 September 2017.

Inpress

- inpressbooks.co.uk
- Newcastle | Founded 2002

Inpress is the UK's specialist in selling books produced by independent publishers. Since 2002, they have worked to support innovative, literary publishers across the UK and Ireland, delivering their fiction, poetry and non-fiction to book lovers worldwide. They bring painstakingly-created, innovative and outside-of-the-mainstream books together in one place.

Modern Poetry in Translation

- mptmagazine.com
- Oxford | Founded 1965
- Editor: Sasha Dugdale; Managing Editor: Debbie DeKock; Digital Manager: Ed Cottrell
- Anthologies, *Modern Poetry in Translation* (magazine)

Modern Poetry in Translation publishes world poetry in translation. It is the only magazine in the English-speaking world to focus on poetry in translation and over the fifty years since it was founded by Ted Hughes and Danny Weissbort it has published and established the reputation of many world poets in English translation, including Yehuda Amichai, Miroslav Holub and Ingeborg Bachmann. It currently publishes a beautiful and addictive magazine three times a year. Each magazine includes a focus section on a certain culture or poetics. Recent focuses include: African language poetry, Brazilian poetry and refugee poetry. *Modern Poetry in Translation* also has a digital programme including podcasts of readings, e-letters, blogs and extra online material, and a highly-successful translation workshop, suitable for all writers with or without knowledge of another language. In recent issues we have published writers as diverse as Korean Kim Hyesoon, Ethiopian Bewketu Seyoum and Macedonian Nikola Madzirov as well as a number of UK poets writing on translation, including Viduan Ravinthiran and Inua Ellams, Pascale Petit and Carola Luther. Subscribe to our e-letter or follow us on Facebook or twitter for more information.

Poetry Archive

- poetryarchive.org.uk
- London | Founded 1999

The Poetry Archive is a not-for-profit organisation which exists to make poetry accessible, relevant and enjoyable to a large audience. Their website offers free access to a huge and growing range of high-quality recordings of English-language poets reading their own work. Many more recordings are available to purchase as digital downloads.

The Poetry Library

- poetrylibrary.org.uk | info@poetrylibrary.org.uk
- Poetry Library, Level 5 Royal Festival Hall, London SE1 8XX
- London | Founded 1953
- Poetry Librarian: Chris McCabe

The Poetry Library is the world's largest English language collection of modern and contemporary poetry and aims to stock all poetry titles published in the UK with a representation of work from other countries. Open Tuesday – Sunday, it is free to join on proof of UK address. The library runs a free monthly event series called Special Edition as well as a programme of exhibitions throughout the year. Proposals are welcome for both. The library's website at www.poetrylibrary.org.uk is a great way to see at glance what events are taking place across the UK (visitors can upload their own poetry events) and its digital archive at www.poetrymagazines.org.uk is a free database of contemporary poems from UK magazines.

The Poetry School

- poetryschool.com | administration@poetryschool.com
- 81 Lambeth Walk, London SE11 6DX
- London / National | Founded 1997
- Executive Director: Sally Carruthers; Creative Director: Julia Bird

The Poetry School was founded in 1997 by poets Jane Duran, Mimi Khalvati and Pascale Petit. Since our earliest years, our courses and activities have encouraged poets and poetry to flourish, and we count many successful publishing and performing writers amongst our past and current students. Students, tutors and staff are all at different stages with their poetry. We have a wide variety of skills and interests, but all of us share a desire to improve our skills, expand our horizons and develop an audience for our work within a community of poets.

The Poetry Society

- poetrysociety.org.uk | info@poetrysociety.org.uk
- 22 Betterton Street, London WC2H 9BX
- London | Founded 1909
- Director: Judith Palmer; The Poetry Review Editor: Maurice Riordan; Membership Manager: Paul McGrane

- Anthologies, Free competition-winner anthologies, Poetry News (members' newsletter), *The Poetry Review* (magazine)
- Submissions welcome for *The Poetry Review*. See guidelines on the website. Plus: Competitions for adults and young people (e.g. National Poetry Competition); and member-only submissions and competitions (e.g. *Poetry News*).

The Poetry Society was founded in 1909 to promote "a more general recognition and appreciation of poetry". Since then, it has grown into one of Britain's most dynamic arts organisations, representing British poetry both nationally and internationally. Today it has more than 4000 members worldwide and publishes the leading poetry magazine, *The Poetry Review*. With innovative education and commissioning programmes and a packed calendar of performances, readings and competitions, The Poetry Society champions poetry for all ages. As well as the Foyle Young Poets of the Year Award, The Poetry Society runs the National Poetry Competition, one of the world's longest-running and most prestigious prizes for an individual poem, and the Ted Hughes Award for New Work in Poetry – the prize founded by Carol Ann Duffy from her honorarium as Poet Laureate.

Poetry Translation Centre

- poetrytranslation.org | info@poetrytranslation.org
- London | Founded 2004
- Artistic Director: Sarah Maguire; Managing Director: Erica Jarnes; Communications Manager: Bern Roche Farrelly
- Single-Author Collections, Chapbooks
- Unsolicited submissions not currently accepted.

The Poetry Translation Centre was established by poet Sarah Maguire in 2004 to translate contemporary poetry from Africa,

Asia and Latin America to a high literary standard.Poetry thrives on translation: it's impossible to imagine English poetry without it. From Chaucer, via Wyatt, Dryden and Pope, to Ezra Pound's Cathay, translation has been its life-blood. But English poetry has yet to engage with the rich poetic traditions of the many languages now spoken in the UK; for Islamic communities in particular, poetry is a particularly significant art form. Our work aims to redress that deficiency.By making their poetry at home in English, we aim to celebrate the cultures of communities that are frequently neglected and abused in the UK, inviting them to play a vital role in British cultural life.

Tower Poetry

- towerpoetry.org.uk | info@towerpoetry.org.uk
- Oxford | Founded 2000
- Administrator: Kathryn Grant
- Pamphlets, Anthologies
- Unsolicited submissions not currently accepted.

Tower Poetry exists to encourage and challenge everyone who reads or writes poetry. Funded by a generous bequest to Christ Church, University of Oxford, by the late Christopher Tower, the aims of Tower Poetry are: to stimulate an enjoyment and critical appreciation of poetry, particularly among young people in education, and to challenge people to write their own poetry. Creative writing should be a central element in literary education, and learning about writing poetry can help students to think about ways of reading poetry. Every year an anthology from the competition's winning entries is published as well as anthologies from the bi-annual Summer Schools.

Creative Writing Courses

List of Organisations Offering Creative Writing Poetry Courses

If you wish to be added to these listings or are interested in advertising, please contact us on poetrybookfair@gmail.com

Arvon
Faber Academy
The Poetry School

Universities:

Aberdeen
Anglia Ruskin
Bath Spa
Birbeck
Birmingham
Bolton
Brighton
Bristol
Brunel
Cardiff Metropolitan
Cardiff
Chichester
Durham
Edinburgh
Exeter
Gloucester
Goldsmiths
Keele
Kent
Kingston
Lancaster
Leeds Trinity
Leicester
London South Bank
Loughborough
Manchester (Centre for New Writing)
Northumbria
Nottingham Trent
Oxford Brookes
Plymouth
Queens Belfast
Roehampton
Royal Holloway
St Andrews
Stirling
Surrey
Sussex
Swansea
UEA
Hertfordshire
Newcastle
Nottingham
Winchester
York St Johns

THE POETRY SCHOOL
WHERE POETRY HAPPENS
The Poetry School is a lifeline
for ordinary people for whom poetry is the thing that sustains them. We may never be famous, we may never even be published but
the Poetry School give us the
opportunity to come together with likeminded people and realise that we are not alone, that our solitary efforts at writing have a value and purpose.
The Poetry School nourishes and nurtures whatever abilities we have and gives support and encouragement to our work and therefore to us as individuals.
It reaches people from all walks of life,
there is no other organisation like it,
it is needed.
Poetry School student, Summer 2015
New programmes every September, January and May
Come and join us – www.poetryschool.com